# UNDERSTANDING
# IRIS MURDOCH

# Understanding Contemporary British Literature

**Matthew J. Bruccoli,** *Editor*

**Understanding Graham Greene**
by R. H. Miller

**Understanding Doris Lessing**
by Jean Pickering

**Understanding Arnold Wesker**
by Robert Wilcher

**Understanding Kingsley Amis**
by Merritt Moseley

**Understanding Iris Murdoch**
by Cheryl K. Bove

# UNDERSTANDING

# Iris
# MURDOCH

by CHERYL K. BOVE

UNIVERSITY OF SOUTH CAROLINA PRESS

Copyright © 1993 University of South Carolina

Published in Columbia, South Carolina, by the
University of South Carolina Press

Manufactured in the United States of America

**Library of Congress Cataloging-in-Publication Data**

Bove, Cheryl Browning, 1944–
    Understanding Iris Murdoch / by Cheryl K. Bove.
       p.    cm. — (Understanding contemporary British literature)
    Includes bibliographical references and index.
    ISBN 0–87249–876–X
    1. Murdoch, Iris—Criticism and interpretation.  I. Title.
  II. Series.
PR6063.U7Z594   1993                    92–35180
823'.914—dc20

*For*

*my family*

# CONTENTS

# EDITOR'S PREFACE

*Understanding Contemporary British Literature* has been planned as a series of guides or companions for students as well as good nonacademic readers. The editor and publisher perceive a need for these volumes because much of the influential contemporary literature makes special demands. Uninitiated readers encounter difficulty in approaching works that depart from the traditional forms and techniques of prose and poetry. Literature relies on conventions, but the conventions keep evolving; new writers form their own conventions— which in time may become familiar. Put simply, *UCBL* provides instruction in how to read certain contemporary writers—identifying and explicating their material, themes, use of language, point of view, structures, symbolism, and responses to experience.

The word *understanding* in the series title was deliberately chosen. Many willing readers lack an adequate understanding of how contemporary literature works; that is, what the author is attempting to express and the means by which it is conveyed. Although the criticism and analysis in the series have been aimed at a level of general accessibility, these introductory volumes are meant to be applied in conjunction with the works they cover. Thus they do not provide a substitute for the works and authors they introduce, but rather prepare the reader for more profitable literary experiences.

M. J. B.

# UNDERSTANDING
# IRIS MURDOCH

# CHAPTER ONE

# The Modern Realist

## Career

Iris Murdoch is Britain's most critically acclaimed living writer. She received the Black Memorial Prize for *The Black Prince*, the Whitbread Literary Award for Fiction for *The Sacred and Profane Love Machine*, and the Booker McConnell Prize for *The Sea, The Sea*. She was named Dame of the Order of the British Empire in 1987, made a Companion of Literature by the Royal Society of Literature in 1987, and awarded the National Arts Club's (New York) Medal of Honor for Literature in 1990. A prolific writer, Murdoch has published twenty-four novels, five plays, four books of philosophy, a short story, a volume of poetry, essays on philosophy and aesthetics, and a libretto for William Mathias's opera *The Servants*, which is based on her play *The Servants and the Snow*.

Born in Dublin to Anglo-Irish parents on July 15, 1919, Murdoch moved to London with her parents at an early age but returned to Ireland frequently to visit relatives. She describes her father, a civil servant, as a quiet, good man who loved books.[1] Her mother was trained for the opera before she was married, and music is a viable element in Murdoch's life and in the lives of her characters. She attended Badminton School in Bristol, which she recalls as being "rather left-wing" with "enlightened liberal views,"[2] and studied "Greats" (Latin and Greek languages, literature, history and philosophy) at Somerville College, Oxford. After receiving a first-class degree in 1942, she was conscripted into the civil service as an assistant principal in the Treasury. Growing up in the Hammersmith and West Chiswick districts of London, working in London during the Second World War, and maintaining a Kensington residence while living in Oxford have provided Murdoch with a familiarity with London's museums, parks, and river areas; these London associations are brilliantly detailed in her novels.

Murdoch also worked as an administrative officer with the United Nations Relief and Rehabilitation Administration in London, Belgium, and Austria from 1944 to 1946. Her experiences in that work find their way into her novels through the displaced Eastern Europeans appearing in *The Flight from the Enchanter, The Time of the Angels,* and *Nuns and Soldiers.* When she was in Belgium after the war she was caught up in the excitement about existentialism, a philosophy which emphasizes individual freedom and action, and was able, for the first time, to obtain works by Jean-Paul Sartre, the leading French existentialist. Sartre's ethics are based on an individual's action, and his novels develop the isolation and angst felt by the existential hero. Murdoch met Sartre and also became friends with Raymond Queneau, a French novelist and poet to whom she dedicated *Under the Net;* this time of her life would reawaken a love for philosophy and affect the direction of her career.[3] In her first published work, *Sartre: Romantic Rationalist*, she discussed Sartre's aesthetics and showed his intent to convey his political vision through his novels.[4] While many critics began associating Murdoch with existentialism after the publication of this work and her first novel, *Under the Net*, she distanced herself from existentialism early in her career and makes it clear in her study of Sartre's novels that she does not think he presents realistic characterization, a fundamental requirement in her aesthetics.

Her fluency in French also brought Murdoch into contact with the writing of the French mystic Simone Weil, whose work with ethics has had a pronounced effect on Murdoch's vision, particularly in her use of paying attention to others as a means of moral improvement and the idea of suffering as a form of consolation rather than as a means of purification.[5]

Following the war, Murdoch received a grant for graduate work in the United States but was refused a student visa because she had briefly been a member of the Communist party while at Oxford. Instead she accepted the Sarah Smithson Studentship in philosophy at Newnham College, Cambridge, where philosophy was still under the influence of the philosopher Ludwig Wittgenstein, whose work *Tractatus* profoundly influenced logical positivism. In 1948 she was named a fellow of St. Anne's College, Oxford, where she taught philosophy. Oxford philosophy emphasized linguistic analysis, and its influence does appear in her novels, primarily through discussions about the inadequacy of language for conveying truth;

however, Murdoch prefers moral philosophy. When she retired from full-time teaching in 1963 to devote more time to her writing, she was named an honorary fellow of St. Anne's College. In 1956 she married the critic John Bayley, who has recently retired as Warton Professor of English, St. Catherine's College, Oxford. The Bayleys live in north Oxford and keep a flat in the Kensington area of London.

### Overview

Iris Murdoch writes in the English realist tradition, so it is not surprising that her novels are filled with the upper-middle-class intellectuals and artists who form her world. She has stated her admiration for the great nineteenth-century realists, and her writing has been compared to that of Fyodor Dostoevsky and George Eliot.[6] She admits that Dostoevsky's work, which exhibits the struggle between good and evil, influenced and inspired her writing.[7] The grand vision of Tolstoy is especially evident in her later works, which have variety of detail and veracity in character.

An emphasis on characterization has always been a primary concern in Murdoch's aesthetics. Early in her writing career (1959) she stated that the greatest problem confronting the modern novelist was the creation of character.[8] A decade later, in an interview with W. K. Rose, she indicated her identification with the English realist tradition and restated her desire to create "real, free characters."[9] A careful study of Murdoch's critical writings and novels reveals her continued interest in characterization; it has become the basis of both her contribution to the development of the novel and the means by which she advances her moral philosophy.

Her moral philosophy and characterization reflect Murdoch's position as a Platonist. She believes that truth and vision are illusive and that individuals are relegated to an illusory life and have only intimations of truth.[10] Her characters display an awareness of truth which is commensurate with their spiritual development. Because the virtuous perceive a higher level of truth than ordinary individuals, Murdoch proposes a means for moral improvement and increased knowledge through Simone Weil's idea of attention. People can come closer to truth if they attend properly to the world and those about them. By stressing the interrelation of aesthetics, moral philosophy, and truth, Murdoch indicates the possibilities of illumination and the consequences of solipsism for both the artist who would convey truth and the reader who would perceive it.

For Murdoch, the modern individual's failure to recognize the interrelated structure of people and events in his or her life is principally a moral failure. One of her characters calls this failure "a massive lack of connection with the world."[11] Only those who are able to lose themselves and attend diligently to the concerns of others are capable of moral advancement. She accepts the Freudian explanation of the psyche as egoistic and believes the natural inclination of the psyche is for consolation and protection. Because of egoism, a spiritual void in the Western consciousness, and the increasing inadequacy of language for communication, the modern individual often recognizes others only as extentions of the self. As a result, the individual remains in a state of spiritual immaturity, with his or her consciousness clouded by illusion. In order to gain some intuitions of truth, one must continually reject the attractions of egoism. But because selflessness is against human nature, few can perfect themselves enough for complete vision, and there are limited prospects for sainthood in this life. Indeed, most of Murdoch's characters are self-interested and egoistic.

Part of the explanation for the modern individual's anxiety and dread is the contingent and accidental nature of life. Daily reminders of one's inability to control one's life have left the individual feeling insecure and unstable. For Murdoch, accidental occurrences are not simply complexities placed in novels to resolve plot. Accidents of chance occur because they actually are a part of life. As Bradley Pearson of *The Black Prince* explains, "life is horrible, without metaphysical sense, wrecked by chance, pain and the close prospect of death (p. 58)."[12] His metaphysical assessment is quite bleak: "Always a world of fear and horror lies but a millimetre away. Any man, even the greatest, can be broken in a moment and has no refuge" (p. xviii).

The accidental and contingent features of human existence are a common theme in all Murdoch novels; she reiterates that life is horrible, life is a muddle, and one's existence has no pattern. For twentieth-century individuals, who have relied so extensively on reason to gain the limited control that they possess over their lives, these utterances are alarming. Murdoch also juxtaposes the conventional with the totalitarian again and again in her novels, showing that, finally, reason cannot replace religion as a consolation for life's occurrences; it fails to control or explain them away or to preclude their occasion.

One novel that stresses the contingent features of human existence is *An Accidental Man* (1971). The title refers to Austin Gibson-Grey, who identifies himself as both accidental man and victim,[13] but these features also extend to his fellow characters, and the novel abounds in accidental signs and occasions. Austin is typical of the muddlers in Murdochland. He has two wives who die accidental deaths; he kills a six-year-old girl while driving under the influence of alcohol, smashes the skull of this girl's stepfather and thereby alters his personality, and is without a job or pension. Austin's view of life is not surprising: "Life . . . [is] misery and muddle, it . . . [is] misery and muddle" (p. 111).

Tragic occasions such as those which bring many characters to their deaths continually remind Murdoch's readers of their vulnerability. In the past, people had faith as a consolation for suffering and as an incentive for moral behavior. Now a firm conviction of a better afterlife no longer exists. Murdoch regrets this loss of common background and the resulting moral breakdown; instead, she would promote acting correctly without the consolation of punishment or reward in the afterlife. The effects of loss of faith on one's consciousness and morality are often discussed in Murdoch novels where those who no longer believe in a traditional God suffer the pain of His withdrawal and continually search for a suitable replacement.

## UNDERSTANDING IRIS MURDOCH

Perhaps Marcus Fisher's book in *The Time of the Angels,* which he calls "a philosophical treatise upon morality in a secular age,"[14] is itself symptomatic of the problem of loss of faith for the Western consciousness. The book, which Marcus had intended, so unlike other philosophical works, to be absolutely lucid, eventually degenerates into a confusion of unconnected aphorisms. This aphoristic style recalls Nietzsche's declaration of the death of God, and the confusion shows the modern individual's reaction to this pronouncement. Religion had provided a consolation for the horrors of the world; now metaphysical concerns yield either anxiety or substitute gods such as materialism.

In *The Philosopher's Pupil,* this time in history, when individuals no longer possess a firm belief in God and are unable to function without a suitable substitute, is called "the time of the angels" (p. 187). In both *The Time of the Angels* and *The Philosopher's Pupil,* humankind's present state is referred to as being an interregnum in which the loss of faith has not been replaced by a belief of substance capable of supporting sustained morality. Father Jacoby and the philosopher John Robert Rozanov discuss this interregnum in *The Philosopher's Pupil.* This "time of the angels" refers to the age in which people believe in spirit (angels) without believing in God (p. 187). In this case, Father Jacoby hopes that humankind will hang on "until religion can change itself into something we can believe in" (p. 187), but elsewhere Murdoch is more pessimistic. The characters in *The Time of the Angels* exist in a literal wasteland in war-torn London in a spiritual lethargy caused by their mutual loss of faith. Carel Fisher, the atheistic

## THE MODERN REALIST

Anglican priest to a parish whose buildings are condemned and will soon be demolished, is the fisher king whose ailment will never be healed; consequently, spiritual prosperity cannot return to his parish.

Another factor contributing to the substance of an individual's consciousness is his or her historic past, including both past events and heritage. Generally Murdoch's characters are fully aware that their pasts figure prominently in their present lives. Rachel Baffin points this out to Bradley Pearson in *The Black Prince:* "One is responsible for one's actions, and one's past does belong to one. You can't blot it out by entering a dream world and decreeing that life began yesterday. You can't make yourself into a new person overnight . . ." (p. 310).

Hilary Burde of *A World Child* is another character who exemplifies the relation between the past and the present. Hilary was an orphanage child, had had a hideous home life, and felt he was unlovable.[15] Eventually he was salvaged by a wonderful schoolmaster, Mr. Osmand, who gave him his full attention and developed Hilary's inclination for languages. Hilary went on to Oxford, studied French and Italian; learned Spanish, Modern Greek, and Russian; won every prize he went for; got one of the top firsts of his year; and was elected to a college fellowship (p. 24).

Hilary's interpersonal relationships, however, are maimed by his past. He fell in love with Anne Jopling, the wife of his best friend, Gunnar, had an affair with her, and was responsible for the deaths of Anne and her unborn child. When Gunnar encounters Hilary twenty years later, he remains driven by his hatred for Hilary. Lady Kitty, Gunnar's present wife, explains their situation: "Our love has always been crippled, damaged, because I could not get in to the place where he was suffering and help him. And I want . . . to see him let go of the past, become free, able to come forward into the future with me with a whole heart" (p. 241). But Hilary has no means to free either Gunnar or himself from the past and will continue the cycle in his responsibility for Lady Kitty's death. Bereft of love as a child, he communicates in a way that is merely mechanical; he cannot establish any relations with Gunnar, and his attempts to do so through Lady Kitty are misinterpreted.

One character who resents his nationality is Emmanuel (Emma) Scarlett-Taylor, a history scholar in *The Philosopher's Pupil*. Emma's Irishness is evident as soon as he opens his mouth, and, much to his exasperation, all new acquaintances remark: "You're Irish?" (p. 124). But, in fact, Emma "hated, with all his heart and soul, Ireland, the Irish, and himself" (p. 122). He saw himself in others' eyes, "as he did for the moment in his own, as a lonely man, with no connections, no relations, no friends . . ." (p. 353).

While some characters are entirely conscious of the past as having a bearing on their present situations, other characters suffer from their refusal to identify with a homeland or with their nationalities. For example, the Count (Wojciech Szczepanski) from *Nuns and Soldiers* feels troubled by and alienated from British society and customs because of his persistent attachment to the conventions of Poland. The Count "passed his childhood in an ardent endeavour to be English, tormented by his father and unable to communicate with his mother."[16] He stubbornly refused to learn Polish, closing his

## THE MODERN REALIST

mind to stories of the destruction of Warsaw and the massacre of two hundred thousand Poles (pp. 9–10). His only ''ambition was to pass his exams and be an ordinary English Schoolboy'' (p. 10). But somehow his Polishness could not be overcome: ''For all his efforts to be English he had a slight foreign accent. And he increasingly felt, in every cell of his being, an alien'' (p. 11). After his mother died he began slowly to accept his heritage. He learned Polish and decided he must visit Warsaw, although the thought of doing so sickened him with anticipation and fear. For the Count, Poland became a universal symbol of struggle against oppression: ''He connected in his mind this ideal symbolic Poland with the sufferings of oppressed people everywhere . . .'' (p. 39). When the Count finally embraces the national spirit which he had rejected as a child, he gains a sense of purpose in his life.

For the Count, as well as for other immigrants in Murdoch novels, the use of native language is an integral part of national essence. In fact, language has a far-reaching impact on all Murdoch characters, for communication is a primary theme in her works. Again and again characters find that they are unable to talk, possess no vocabulary to express what they want to say, or lack common grounds for communication. Even subgroups within the same language (i.e., different social classes, ethnic groups, and professional groups) have semantic difficulties when speaking to someone outside of the group. But by far the most pervasive belief expressed among Murdoch characters is that any attempt to communicate by language, written or spoken, results in lies. This view can be attributed in part to Murdoch's connection with linguistic analysis.

## UNDERSTANDING IRIS MURDOCH

Some Murdoch characters suffer from such severe linguistic alienation that they are unable to communicate, even with members of their own families, without external stimulus. Several characters in *The Philosopher's Pupil* display this symptom. Alex McCaffrey is unable to act naturally with her own children and grandchild on land but is able to do so while swimming at the Ennistone outdoor pool. Even the philosopher John Robert Rozanov can only hold a real conversation with his granddaughter, Hattie, when both are tipsy. Yet another character to use liquor as a speech enhancer is Edgar Demornay in *The Sacred and Profane Love Machine:* "Could I have some more Scotch? I can't converse without it these days," Edgar tells his friend Montague Small.[17]

Another common feature of communication breakdown is the inability to say what one means, either through lack of communication skills or because there are no words to express what is meant. In *The Black Prince* Bradley Pearson aptly notes that "one soon finds out how puny is one's power to describe or to connect" (p. 331). And Julian Baffin, writing a farewell letter to him, finds herself incapable of explaining her feelings properly (p. 320).

Murdoch partially blames this loss of common background for the increasing inadequacy of language for communication. People who have different natures, who see the world differently, have no common semantic base. This point is made in several novels where the bereaved cannot communicate with the unbereaved. One example of lack of common experience leading to communication failure takes place in *An Accidental Man*. After Austin Gibson-Grey runs over and kills

## THE MODERN REALIST

the only child of Mrs. Monkley, Austin's brother, Matthew, and social worker Mavis Argyll attend the girl's funeral and return with the Monkleys to their house for tea. When Matthew tries to comfort Mrs. Monkley, Mavis realizes that he cannot communicate with her: "He is putting words together, thought Mavis. What she says is true, what he says is false. It is not his fault. A real experience of death isolates one absolutely. The bereaved cannot communicate with the unbereaved" (p. 191).

Norah Shadox Brown's conversation with the Bishop in *The Time of the Angels* is yet another illustration of communication failure due to diverse backgrounds. Norah, whose remarks connect her with linguistic analysis, wants things said in "plain terms" (p. 21) and regards "all subtleties as falsehoods" (p. 14). Unwilling to attend to the multivarious detail separating each person's experience, Norah refuses to listen to the Bishop's statements concerning the personal nature of faith. Where doubts of faith are concerned, Norah insists that "[a] spade must be called a spade" (p. 99). Because generalizations do not give full justice to the various details which surround any circumstance, even the loss of faith of an Anglican priest, it is impossible to speak in "plain terms."

The recurring concept of the impossibility of telling the truth expresses a breakdown in the function of language which is evident in all of Murdoch's novels. Bradley Pearson of *The Black Prince* suggests the reasoning behind the belief that one can utter only lies: "How can one describe a human being 'justly'? . . . How can these statements not be false? Even 'I am tall' has a context. . . . We defend ourselves by descriptions and tame the world by generalizing'' (p. 58). Because the world is in many ways more various and rich with detail than anyone can imagine or describe, and because every situation possesses factors of which one is unaware, something less than the truth is conveyed by any statement.

Given the dread and anxiety caused by the factors bearing on an individual's consciousness, Murdoch believes people possess a natural form of defense within the psyche which enables them to live in the world of contingency and chance by directing their behavior in terms of ego-satisfaction. This belief is established through characters such as Bradley Pearson, who recognizes the strong attraction of consolation: "The natural tendency of the human soul is towards the protection of the ego" (*The Black Prince,* p. 152). Another character, identified only as Frances's tall son in *The Red and the Green,* believes that "hardly anything we do is really accidental. . . . Nearly everything we do is our unconscious mind, only we don't know."[18]

Perhaps Murdoch comes closest to defining the interrelated nature of her concept of consciousness, that eclectic collection of experience and essence which she feels directs an individual's choices, when Bradley Pearson discusses the difficulty of changing human consciousness (and thus altering action) in *The Black Prince:*

> In fact the problem remains unclarified because no
> philosopher and hardly any novelist has ever managed
> to explain what that weird stuff, human consciousness,
> is really made of. Body, external objects, darty memo-

ries, warm fantasies, other minds, guilt, fear, hesita-
tion, lies, glees, doles, breathtaking pains, a thousand
things which words can only fumble at, coexist, many
fused together in a single unit of consciousness. How
human responsibility is possible at all could well puzzle an extra-galactic student of this weird method of
proceeding through time. How can such a thing be
tinkered with and improved, how can one change the
quality of consciousness? (p. 157)

Here, through Pearson, Murdoch states the pragmatic problem
implied by her moral philosophy, that of improving the moral
nature of mankind.

This problem poses the central issue of Iris Murdoch's
moral philosophy: she believes the study of ethics should not
only address moral improvement but should actually present a
moral philosophy which one could live by. *The Sovereignty of
Good* proposes the means for individual perfection by connecting virtue and truth and love. Although often enigmatic in her
explanations, Murdoch does give the reader a sense of direction here: "Where virtue is concerned we often apprehend
more than we clearly understand and *grow by looking.*"[19]
Such just and attentive looking is seen as an exercise of love.
Here beauty and art can act as incentives for moral perfection.
In an individual's apprehension of nature or art (which reflects, more closely than nature, the reality of life), one can
momentarily forget oneself.[20] Any movement away from the
self is seen as moral improvement.

Iris Murdoch demonstrates moral awareness in her novels
through her characterization. Most of her characters, like real

people, are egoistic and have corresponding limited vision. But some few characters strive toward the good and have intimations of truth and correct vision. Such characters are seldom strong characters because her good are pictured as humble.[21] Murdoch has also indicated the difficulty of presenting interesting good characters because they are not assertive.[22] However, her novels present a convincing portrait of the good person through several characters who approach goodness.[23] These characters are creative, often artists or scholars who have fully developed their spiritual aspects through sublimation of self, and they possess an acute sense of moral awareness which enables them to recognize the interconnectedness of all things. The good may or may not believe in God, but often they have eclectic religious beliefs, mixing Christian ideals with Buddhist tenets. For example, they see unity in all life and strive for the harmony of all living things. Humility is their prime virtue.[24] Because they are not worldly and are not looking for earthly consolations or rewards, these characters are often viewed as failures by their materialistic and ego-ridden fellow characters.

While Murdoch's good characters may possess power, they do not use it to gain selfish ends, for manipulation and power-wielding are worldly concerns which desecrate spirituality. Instead, they display a just apprehension of others. Their moral vision precedes right action, which separates them from those characters who may gain some knowledge but who choose to reject the spiritual aspirations of the good for the "happiness" offered by worldly attachments.[25] Elizabeth Dipple develops an extensive definition of the "character of the good'' in her study *Iris Murdoch: Work for the Spirit*.[26] According to Dipple, ''the character of the good in Murdoch's fiction will direct himself towards the futile aim of good, act for nothing [and] acknowledge that sainthood is impossible and that we will never know much.''[27] And she identifies the ''stable qualities'' which this character possesses: ''to expect nothing, to avoid theorizing, to renounce brief dazzlement and imagery, [and] to abjure distracting magics.''[28]

Although Murdoch believes that moral improvement is extremely difficult and that the good is nearly unattainable, her vision is not without optimism. Recognizing that people exist other than as extensions of oneself changes the configuration of elements comprising the basis for choice. Any attention which moves one in the direction of awareness of others also moves one away from self and brings about moral improvement. Her novels continue to center on art and love because she maintains that great art or intense love can give intimations of truth (*The Black Prince*, p. 158), and move one toward moral perfection.

For Murdoch, the artist has a moral task to present a just vision of reality, one which includes free and various characters. She also places a great trust in her readers, encouraging them to strive against the interference of egoism in their perception of truth in art and in life. One cannot read Murdoch's novels without becoming aware of the far-reaching, damaging effects of egoism. Because she provides a picture of how people actually are, the reader cannot fail to notice how people ought to be. Murdoch's vision admonishes her readers to attend to others, to really *see* them as distinct and separate individuals with rights of their own; thus her art not only contributes to the development of the novel, but it advances the human condition as well.

## *Notes*

1. Jeffrey Meyers, "An Interview with Iris Murdoch," *Denver Quarterly* 26, no. 1 (Summer 1991): 103.

2. Ibid., p. 104.

3. W. K. Rose, "Iris Murdoch, informally," *London Magazine* 8 (June 1968): 63.

4. See chapter two for a fuller discussion of this work under the section entitled "Sartre: Romantic Rationalist."

5. See A. S. Byatt's discussion of Simone Weil's influence on Iris Murdoch's work in *Degrees of Freedom: The Novels of Iris Murdoch* (London: Chatto & Windus, 1965).

6. Peter Conradi, *Iris Murdoch: The Saint and the Artist* (New York: St. Martin's Press, 1986), p. 22.

7. "The World-Wide Significance of Dostoevsky," *Soviet Literature* 12, no. 405 (1981): 130.

8. Iris Murdoch, "The Sublime and Beautiful Revisited," *Yale Review* 49 (December 1959): 247.

9. Rose, p. 73.

10. See chapter two for a fuller discussion of Murdoch's Platonism, particularly the section entitled "The Sovereignty of Good."

11. Iris Murdoch, *The Philosopher's Pupil* (London: Chatto & Windus, 1983), p. 229. Subsequent references to this work are noted parenthetically in the text.

12. Iris Murdoch, *The Black Prince* (New York: Viking Press, 1973), p. 58; subsequent references to this work are noted parenthetically in the text.

13. Iris Murdoch, *An Accidental Man* (New York: Viking Press, 1971), p. 424; subsequent references to this work are noted parenthetically in the text.

## THE MODERN REALIST

14. Iris Murdoch, *The Time of the Angels* (New York: Viking Press, 1969), p. 15; subsequent references to this work are noted parenthetically in the text.

15. Iris Murdoch, *A World Child* (New York: Viking Press, 1975), p. 18; subsequent references to this work are noted parenthetically in the text.

16. Iris Murdoch, *Nuns and Soldiers* (New York: Viking Press, 1980), p. 11; subsequent references to this work are noted parenthetically in the text.

17. Iris Murdoch, *The Sacred and Profane Love Machine* (New York: Viking Press, 1974), p. 42, subsequent references to this work are noted parenthetically in the text.

18. Iris Murdoch, *The Red and the Green* (New York: Viking Press, 1965), p. 309; subsequent references to this work are noted parenthetically in the text.

19. Iris Murdoch, "The Idea of Perfection," in *The Sovereignty of Good* (New York: Schocken Books, 1970), p. 31.

20. Iris Murdoch, "The Sovereignty of Good Over Other Concepts," in *The Sovereignty of Good* (New York: Schocken Books, 1970), p. 90; subsequent references to this work are noted parenthetically in the text.

21. See the discussion about Tallis Browne of *A Fairly Honourable Defeat* in chapter three. Although muddled and apparently ineffective, Browne is one of Murdoch's few saints. Other "good" characters include Bledyard (*The Sandcastle*), William Eastcote (*The Philosopher's Pupil*), Brendan Craddock (*Henry and Cato*), and Hugo Belfounder (*Under the Net*).

22. Barbara Stevens Heusel, "An Interview with Iris Murdoch," *University of Windsor Review* 1 (Spring 1965): 12.

23. Several nearly good characters include Denis Nolan (*The Unicorn*), Ann Peronett (*An Unofficial Rose*), and Anne Cavidge (*Nuns and Soldiers*).

24. Murdoch defines humility as "selfless respect for reality and one of the most difficult and central of all virtues" in *The Fire and the Sun: Why Plato Banished the Artists* (Oxford: Oxford University Press, 1977), p. 95.

25. Effingham Cooper has an epiphany following a near death experience in *The Time of the Angels,* but lacks the spirituality to sustain his vision and returns to his life of egoism.

26. Elizabeth Dipple, *Iris Murdoch: Work for the Spirit* (Chicago: University of Chicago Press, 1982), p. 57.

27. Ibid, p. 69.

28. Ibid, p. 57.

# CHAPTER TWO

# Moral Philosophy and Aesthetics

### *Sartre: Romantic Rationalist* (1953)

Iris Murdoch's first published work, *Sartre: Romantic Rationalist,* which provides a viable critical study of Sartre's writings, was recently reissued with a new introduction.[1] In this work she illustrates her interest in the relationship between aesthetics and philosophy, voices her admiration for Jean-Paul Sartre while at the same time distancing herself from his existentialism, and provides the reader with an early view of her aesthetics. Particularly illuminating on her aesthetic position are her discussions about what the novel should and should not be; how characterization should be developed; and why Sartre, although a brilliant thinker, fails as a novelist.

Murdoch indicates the intellectual history which brought Sartre to his vision of the role of the novel, identifying both Marxist and existential traits in his work. Through her criticism of Sartre's ends, she develops a vision of the novel which is decidedly within the realist tradition. But Sartre, well aware of the influence of the novel, turned to it with the interest of

## 21

## MORAL PHILOSOPHY AND AESTHETICS

"a sincere propagandist" and intended to use it for his own political message.[2]

The structuralist debate about the relation of words to reality is important in Murdoch's aesthetics. Language has lost its ability to communicate because individuals no longer possess a shared past (such as belief in God). Murdoch views this loss as tragic, as she explains in *Sartre,* and portrays her characters as suffering from the loss of "common purposes and common values" (p. 33).[3] Painting and literature evidence this linguistic disturbance. Surrealists claimed to be indifferent to art and morality and connected their product with the exploration of the unconscious; their hatred of their society, evident in their art, soon linked them with Marxism (p. 36). The traditional form of the novel was rejected, and James Joyce and Virginia Woolf presented a new reality in their novels through stream of consciousness.

Sartre inherited "much of the spirit of Surrealism" (p. 41) and used the introspective technique of characterization (p. 44). His internal monologue presented past events "as if they were happening now" (p. 46). However, Sartre's main interests were in the ideas which he presented through his characters rather than in the fate of his characters. Murdoch does not believe that presenting character through internal monologue necessarily limits the development of character, but she does feel that care must be taken to present enough material (and the right kind of material) about the character so that the reader does not lose interest in the narrator.

Sartre sets a task for his reader which brings him or her into the novel: "The reader too must be the creator of the novel; his continuing to read it 'properly', that is to enter into it seriously, to 'lend' it his emotions and so on, involves him in a sustained act of faith in the work itself'' (p. 61). The emphasis for the artist and the consumer of art is freedom. The novelist must show the world as it is, ''in the perspectives of a possible change'' (p. 63), and the reader must judge the work independent of ''his resentments, his fears, and his lusts in order to put himself at the peak of his freedom'' (p. 63).

Murdoch also accepts a moral obligation on the part of the artist and the consumer to attend properly to reality in the work of art, but her emphasis is not on freedom in Sartre's sense. For Sartre the novel becomes a political device, and Murdoch does not believe one should write a novel with the intention of making political statements. This difference indicates her reservations about Sartre's writing: his characterization. For when a writer has a political statement in mind, then that writer is less free to present free and various characters without interference from the political message.[4]

While both Sartre and Murdoch connect art with morality, they differ in their methods and their meaning. For Sartre, transmitting the ideological commitment is necessarily a moral act. For Murdoch, a just portrayal of reality is a virtuous act. Although she admires Sartre, she believes that he ultimately fails as a great novelist because he ''has an impatience, which is fatal to a novelist proper, with the *stuff* of human life'' (p. 112). He has no ''apprehension of the absurd irreducible uniqueness of people and of their relations with each other'' (p. 112). In short, he is interested in issues rather than in people; such an interest is more appropriate for the theater

## MORAL PHILOSOPHY AND AESTHETICS

than for the novel. And those who read his novels may be left with "a sense of emptiness" with regard to his characters (p. 114).

### *The Sovereignty of Good* (1967)

*The Sovereignty of Good* contains three essays, "The Idea of Perfection," "On 'God' and 'Good,' " and "The Sovereignty of Good over Other Concepts," in which Murdoch develops her moral philosophy by discussing the importance of inner vision for moral improvement and the place of good in a world which no longer believes in God. Here Murdoch connects great art with the good and intimations of the good with love, freedom, and moral improvement. Although some of the discussion is dated because of the emphasis on existentialism, this work establishes the basis for Murdoch's moral philosophy and aesthetics.

The first essay, "The Idea of Perfection," considers the behaviourist-existentialist view of man presented by most modern philosophers as unrealistic and advances Murdoch's own view of a historical man who experiences moral choice through attention and inner vision. Murdoch does not believe the existential model of individual freedom because she does not think man chooses without reason. She would like to say that "mental concepts enter the sphere of morality" (p. 26) and that choice depends upon our vision of the world. Her view of people as "human historical individuals" helps determine her vision of the world.[5]

She explains how individuals become more virtuous, that is *"grow by looking,"* by relating virtue to linguistic philosophy: "Words . . . have both spatio-temporal and conceptual contexts. We learn through attending to contexts, vocabulary develops through close attention to objects, and we can only understand others if we can to some extent share their contexts" (p. 32). Communication with others requires some common context. Here, as in many of her novels, she praises literature for being a "fundamental aspect of culture" and educating us "in how to picture and understand human situations" (p. 34).[6]

Morality is connected with attention because one can choose only the world which one sees (p. 37). The more one focuses one's attention on the subject at hand, or on another individual, the more one will have an unbiased view of that situation or individual: "If I attend properly I will have no choices and this is the ultimate condition to be aimed at" (p. 40). Goodness, while difficult to explain or define, is connected with knowledge, which can be gained by actually attending to the situation at hand.

The second essay, "On 'God' and 'Good,' " assumes that belief in God is declining and develops an argument for placing Good at the focus of our attention instead. Again Murdoch finds the existing British philosophies inadequate in their treatment of morality and looks for a philosophy which "one could live by" (p. 47); she would like moral philosophy actually to tell us how to improve morally. Murdoch suggests replacing God with Good as the center of an individual's attention because people who focus their attention on valuable things, such as "virtuous people, great art, perhaps . . . the idea of goodness itself," can improve morally (p. 56).

Murdoch finds Freud's view of fallen man "realistic and acceptable," though she asserts that she is not Freudian (p. 51).[7] His description of the psyche explains how it works and can be changed: "He sees the psyche as an egocentric system of quasi-mechanical energy, largely determined by its own individual history, whose natural attachments are sexual, ambiguous, and hard for the subject to understand or control" (p. 51). Murdoch is primarily interested in the workings of the ego, which she believes must be defeated for one to achieve spiritual amelioration.

The enemy of moral excellence is fantasy, which is untruthful and a form of consolation (p. 59). Suffering can be such a consolation because it "can masquerade as a purification" (p. 68). True suffering is almost unbearable, so the human tendency is to make it into something else, a form of consolation, a form of protection from the truth.

These ideas fuse Iris Murdoch's moral philosophy and aesthetics, for beauty and great art are the means for moral improvement. Both the artist and the audience have a responsibility for "unsentimental, detached, unselfish, objective attention," if any truth is to be conveyed (pp. 65–66). Since reality (truth) is the "proper object of love" (p. 68), individuals must rid themselves of fantasy and consolation which give them a false perception of reality.

The final essay, "The Sovereignty of Good Over Other Concepts," continues the development of art as a means for discovering reality and shows the relationship between the proximity of death and truth and the consolation of suffering. Other virtues are defined in terms of Good, and humility is shown as the virtue closest to the Good.

Again Murdoch emphasizes what she believes should be the ends of moral philosophy: "Ethics . . . should be a hypothesis about good conduct and about how this can be achieved" (p. 78). The discussion begins with two fundamental assumptions, one from Freud's description of the psyche and one about her own religious conviction: "Human beings are naturally selfish and . . . human life has no external point" (p. 79).

While normally Platonic in her views, Murdoch admits that she and Plato do not entirely agree about art. Plato saw art as a starting point but came to mistrust it as a "consolation which distorts reality" (p. 88). Murdoch believes that if individuals attend correctly, then great art can give them intimations of truth. She would agree with Plato that few people will ever know truth, but she believes that individuals can move toward moral perfection by just and loving attention to art, which can show them the real and various nature of life.

To remain concerned with the self is to remain in a state of illusion. One of the means of unselfing is the proximity of death. Nearly all of the characters in Murdoch's novels who have near-death experiences realize some truth, even if their spiritual states are such that they cannot maintain this vision and make any real changes in their lives. For example, just before he dies from a heart attack, the poet Lucius Lamb realizes, in one final haiku, that death is a great teacher.[8] And

## MORAL PHILOSOPHY AND AESTHETICS

when trapped in Gunnar's cave with the sea waters rising around him, John Ducane realizes that love, reconciliation, and forgiveness are the true worth in life.[9]

For Murdoch, only through the acceptance of "real death and real chance and real transcience" can one discover what virtue is like. Once one recognizes his or her true place in the universe, his or her lack of worth, one can begin to recognize others and love them: "The acceptance of death is an acceptance of our own nothingness which is an automatic spur to our concern with what is not ourselves" (p. 103). The few places where Murdoch believes virtue can be found are "great art . . . [and] humble people who serve others" (p. 99). Great art can give intimations of the real and various nature of life, and a humble man, "because he sees himself as nothing, can see other things as they are" (pp. 103–04). "The humble man perceives the distance between suffering and death" (p. 104). It is this individual, who recognizes himself or herself as nothing and who may not actually be a good person, who has the possibility of becoming one in Iris Murdoch's moral philosophy (p. 104).

### *The Fire and the Sun: Why Plato Banished the Artists* (1977)

In *The Fire and the Sun,* based on her 1976 Romanés Lecture, Murdoch discusses the roles of the artist and art throughout Plato's writing, compares his ideas with those of Kant and Freud, and then employs Plato's own statements to make the case for art as the means for conveying truth and for spiritual amelioration. In so doing, Murdoch develops her own aesthetics, which are based on Platonic thinking but diverge in the area of art and its relation to moral perfection. Many of these ideas, particularly the role of art in moral perfection, the difficulty of spiritual growth, the connection between awareness and spirituality, and the necessity of humility for goodness, remain in her aesthetics today and are illustrated by her current novels.

Murdoch describes Plato, as revealed in his writings, as serious, religious, and concerned with spiritual salvation. In his Theory of Forms "Plato pictures human life as a pilgrimage from appearance to reality."[10] His famous allegory of the cave presents a method for explaining an individual's state of illusion. The allegory depicts humans as prisoners, chained together, facing the back wall of a cave. They see only shadows of the real world outside the cave; these shadows are reflected by a fire behind them. At this stage of spirituality, the captives see little of reality. But those who grow spiritually are able to turn around and face the fire and have a better glimpse of truth. Only a very few will be capable of actually coming outside the cave to view reality, and it will be almost impossible for these to reach the highest spiritual level where they can actually look at the sun and understand truth (p. 4). The sun, for Plato, "represents the Form of the Good in whose light the truth is seen" (p. 4).

Because Plato was concerned with spiritual salvation, he was intolerant of anything which would give a false view of the world or present life as a consolation. The *Republic* dis-

## MORAL PHILOSOPHY AND AESTHETICS

cusses the importance of didactic art and thus the necessity for censorship of stories about the gods which show them as "undignified and immoral" (p. 5).[11] Plato did approve of art which was quite simple. Didactic poetry was permitted, and hymns to the gods were acceptable, but Plato would ban all representational art (p. 16); it could only present illusion.

Murdoch believes that Freud's ideas about the psyche may have something to tell us about Plato's mistrust of art. Individuals find illusions consoling and hesitate to relinquish them in order to reach a higher spiritual level. The illusions are egoistic, a means of protection. For Plato, "the soul must be saved . . . by the redirection of its energy away from selfish fantasy [ego] toward reality" (p. 38).

According to Murdoch, Plato's connection of the good with the real is "the center of his thought and one of the most fruitful ideas in philosophy" (p. 45). She also makes this concept the center of her own moral philosophy by equating Plato's state of illusion with egoism. Such traits as "obsession, prejudice, envy, anxiety, ignorance, greed, neurosis, and so on . . . *veil* reality" (p. 47). Only by a concentrated moral effort can one rid oneself of these illusions and move in the direction of moral perfection. It is precisely because these traits are consoling and act as a protection for the ego that individuals are so reluctant to let go of them.

While Plato changed his views on many subjects during the course of his writings, Murdoch emphasizes that his views of art and the artist (whom he places at the lowest level of spiritual development) never change. She feels that in many ways Plato's objections to art were on religious grounds.[12] He believed art was dangerous because, by representing the spiritual, art "subtly disguise[d] and trivialize[d] it" (p. 65). His idea of the world of illusion as more attractive and easier to bear than reality is incorporated into Iris Murdoch's moral philosophy and evident in her novels.[13]

Although she would agree with Plato about the dangers of false consolations and illusion, Murdoch would like to develop great art as a means for changing the consciousness of the ego-ridden individual: "Art is far and away the most educational thing we have" (p. 86) and, although it cannot tell the whole of truth, it can "pierce the veil" and point individuals towards reality. Truth is shown by artists such as Shakespeare, who are able to present the immense variety and detail which a just picture of the world requires: "The good artist helps us to see the place of necessity in human life, what must be endured, what makes and breaks, and to purify our imagination so as to contemplate the real world (usually veiled by anxiety and fantasy) including what is terrible and absurd" (p. 80).

### Acastos: Two Platonic Dialogues (1986)

Set in Athens in the late fifth century B.C., *Art and Eros: A Dialogue about Art* was first performed as a National Theatre Platform Performance in February 1980. This dialectic, following Plato's model in dialogues such as *Ion* and *Meno*, presents representative ideas about the value of art and establishes Plato's primary objections to art, which he set forth in the *Republic*, as irreverent and illusory. The youthful fervency of Iris Murdoch's Plato is softened by remarks by an older and

## MORAL PHILOSOPHY AND AESTHETICS

more tolerant Socrates, who sees art as imperfect, since it is created by humans, but worth the effort.

The principals, who have just come from the theater, voice their opinions about drama. Mantias, a political man, does not like plays but goes to the theater to monitor its influence and thinks that art can be used as propaganda.[14] Deximenes, a cynical man, remarks that the theater is magic (p. 12), an idea developed to a greater extent by another Murdoch character, Charles Arrowby, in *The Sea, The Sea*. Callistos, a beautiful youth, is taken in by the dream world of the theater, (pp. 12-13); Acastos, a serious youth, enjoyed the play and was moved by it but doesn't know why (p. 14).

Socrates begins questioning Callistos, trying to refine his definition of art by discussing its merit and usefulness. Throughout the discussion Murdoch interjects Plato's ideas about art and its censorship as shown in the *Republic*. The censorship question also extends into a religious controversy because the *Republic* would censor those passages of Homer which make the gods look foolish; Plato felt these passages promoted loss of faith. Still another religious objection which Plato made about art in the *Republic* concerns idolatry. Since art is imitation, it may be irreverent because one really does not know what the gods are like (p. 15). But Socrates conciliates the religious question through a statement which makes him Iris Murdoch's spokesman: "I think that religion will always be with us, and we shall continually remake it into something we can believe" (p. 40).

While Mantias's argument that art should be censored and be useful to society is upheld by Plato in Book II of the *Republic*, the youthful Plato, the character of this play, brings the discussion to a higher, enigmatic level by claiming that good art is also connected with emotion and Eros. Acastos, rephrasing Plato's ideas to clarify them for himself, finally states the value of art: "Because of this passion, which is a kind of *vision*, artists can see truth and tell truth, they can tell more truth than anyone else, they can *communicate* it" (p. 54). But Plato, ever the absolutist, cannot agree; he sees art as dangerous to philosophy and religion because "it masquerades as the whole truth and makes us content with something less" (p. 54).

Socrates, more accepting than Plato of the infirmities of mankind, agrees that Homer is imperfect and that "not everything connects," but "we are not gods" (p. 62). He makes a closing point, which echoes the connection between truth and love in Murdoch's moral philosophy: "In truly loving each other we learn more perhaps than in all our studies" (p. 65).

*Above the Gods,* the second of the dialectics in *Acastos,* concerns the place of religion in a society in which the traditional belief in the gods no longer exist. The dialectic, set in Athens in the late fifth century B.C., has relevance for that time, when traditional belief in the Greek anthropomorphic gods was declining, and for the present, when modern science and philosophy are demythologizing Christianity. While Iris Murdoch believes in a higher spirit, she does not believe in an afterlife or that God intervenes in one's life.[15] Her moral philosophy suggests replacing God with good, and she wants people to be attracted towards the good; individuals should not act morally for any exterior reason such as the punishment or reward accorded after death. *Above the Gods* addresses both

# MORAL PHILOSOPHY AND AESTHETICS

the difficulty of acting without hope of reward and the grim isolation that may accompany an acceptance of the withdrawal of God.

The dialectic is framed by a religious festival. The characters have just returned from the festival and discover that several of them do not believe in the gods, or at least in the gods as they are presented in mythology. At the end of the discussion, they will join an evening torchlight religious procession, inspired, perhaps, to strive for good.

Antagoras, a sophist, believes that religion is essentially superstition.[16] He views religion as necessary for "a stable and orderly society," thus providing a political argument for keeping it (p. 78). Timorax, a socially conscious youth, believes "religion is *immoral*, it stops people from thinking about how to change society" (p. 80). Acastos agrees with the others to some extent; he, too, does not believe in the old myths and stories, and he admits that "religion does a lot of bad things" (p. 83). But he would like to have religion go on, without the lying, because "religion *contains* morality" (p. 88). He also argues that religion has some worth: "So a religious attitude sees our life as an interconnected whole" (p. 89). Socrates then proposes that someone might believe that the "old stories are not literally true, but that they can *convey* truth" (p. 75). He advocates a good way of life without supernatural beliefs (p. 79), the same argument advanced in other Murdoch philosophy.[17]

Plato enters the discussion and announces that religion must be necessary and certain (p. 98) but that humans do not understand their task. The task is "finding out what's real and responding to it—like when we really see other people and know they exist" (p. 101). Finding the good takes the spirit "above the gods" and connects it with Eros, which Socrates defines as "a holy passionate spirit that seeks for God, what you call Good" (p. 106). Plato believes that goodness and truth come out of the depths of the soul (p. 107) and that people instinctively know good. The real basis of morality, then, is religion, which Plato defines as "the love and worship of the good" (p. 109). So the discussion has come full circle, but the definition has been expanded to include the unattainable good. As far as moral improvement is concerned, Socrates has this advice: "If we do good things which are near to us we may improve a little. . . . Goodness is simple, it's just very difficult" (p. 120).

## Notes

1. Iris Murdoch, *Sartre: Romantic Rationalist* (London: Chatto & Windus, 1987).

2. Iris Murdoch, *Sartre: Romantic Rationalist* (New Haven & London: Yale University Press, 1953), p. x; subsequent references to this work are from this edition and are noted parenthetically in the text.

3. See, for example, the Lusiewicz brothers (*The Flight from the Enchanter*).

4. She comments on her belief that political propaganda is better suited to other genres than the novel in Michael O. Bellamy, "An Interview with Iris Murdoch," *Contemporary Literature* 18, no. 2 (Spring 1977): 129–40.

5. Iris Murdoch, *The Sovereignty of Good* (New York: Schocken Books, 1971), p. 29; subsequent references to this work are noted parenthetically in the text.

# MORAL PHILOSOPHY AND AESTHETICS

6. Iris Murdoch maintains that great art, literature included, can reveal fundamental truths across cultures and generations.

7. See *A Severed Head,* in which Murdoch satirizes Freudian psycho-analytical theory.

8. *Henry and Cato,* p. 364.

9. *The Nice and the Good,* p. 329.

10. Iris Murdoch, *The Fire and the Sun: Why Plato Banished the Artists* (Oxford: Oxford University Press, 1977), p. 2; subsequent references to this work are noted parenthetically in the text.

11. This argument is developed at greater length in *Art and Eros: A Dialogue about Art* (a dialectic in *Acastos*).

12. See *Above the Gods* (a dialectic in *Acastos*) for a further discussion of the importance of religion to Plato.

13. Several characters in Murdoch's novels find truth too difficult to bear and choose instead a mediocre life of illusion: Henry Marshalson (*Henry and Cato*) and Effingham Cooper (*The Unicorn*) are examples.

14. Iris Murdoch, *Art and Eros: A Dialogue about Art,* in *Acastos: Two Platonic Dialogues* (London: Chatto & Windus, 1986), p. 33; subsequent references to this work are noted parenthetically in the text.

15. See Stephen Glover, "Iris Murdoch Talks to Stephen Glover, *New Review* 3, no. 32 (November 1976): 56–59.

16. Iris Murdoch, *Above the Gods: A Dialogue about Religion,* in *Acastos: Two Platonic Dialogues* (London: Chatto & Windus, 1986), p. 75; subsequent references to this work are noted parenthetically in the text.

17. Iris Murdoch, *The Sovereignty of Good* (New York: Schocken Books, 1971); see "On 'God' and 'Good,' " pp. 46–76.

# CHAPTER THREE

# Early Major Works
# (1954–1962)

### *Under the Net* (1954)

*U*nder the Net, Iris Murdoch's first published novel, is a comic adventure featuring the feckless Jake Donaghue, a failed artist and picaresque hero. Donaghue guides the reader on pub crawls through London's financial district and Paris's Left Bank while he searches for meaning and love in his life. Picaresque and existential, *Under the Net* is dedicated to French novelist Raymond Queneau, and Murdoch has admitted his influence in this work, claiming that she was copying him as hard as she could.[1] Yet it is her only clearly derivitive and existential novel, and she never repeats this pattern in her later novels. Nevertheless, *Under the Net* foreshadows her mature works with its fast-paced plot, closely detailed settings, fully developed characters, and attention to moral issues. This novel is also responsible for Murdoch's being typed with the "angry young men" who were also publishing first novels at the same time, John Wain and Kingsley Amis. However, while Murdoch's works always have moral concerns, she does not write antiestablishment novels about social injustice.

The novel's protagonist has much to learn about himself and about life, and he does so with carefree abandon in detailed and specific London and Paris settings. Much of the novel is set in London, particularly the Holborn and financial districts, with their numerous pubs and churches. Though some of the buildings have been replaced with renovation, much of Donaghue's pub crawl with Dave Gellman and Finn can still be traced today: ". . . We approached the Skinners' Arms. This pub stands at the junction of Cannon Street and Queen Victoria Street, under the shadow of St. Mary, Aldermary. We rolled in."[2] Even Donaghue's descriptions of the surrounds of Hugo's flat are accurate nearly forty years after they were written:

> Hugo lived, it appeared, right up above Holborn Viaduct, in a flat perched on top of some office buildings. . . . If you have ever visited the City of London in the evening you will know what an uncanny loneliness possesses these streets which during the day are so busy and noisy. The Viaduct is a dramatic viewpoint. But although we could see for a long way . . . we could see no living being. (p. 99)

Donaghue also follows Murdoch's own Paris haunts in two of the novel's chapters. As noted earlier, she worked with the United Nations Relief and Rehabilitation Agency in Belgium and Austria following the war and spent a considerable amount of time in post-war Paris. Her familiarity with the Left Bank and such public gardens as the Luxembourg and the Tuileries is evident in this novel of her youth.

A rather lazy writer who makes his living translating best-sellers by Jean Pierre Breteuil at the expense of his own artistic talents, Donaghue experiences mixed feelings about Paris. He apparently speaks fluent French, for his dialogue is sprinkled liberally with French phrases, yet he feels himself an outsider, unable to communicate with anyone else in Paris. Murdoch's gift of detailed and close observation superbly conveys the feeling of the frenzied carnivalesque Paris on Bastille Day while Donaghue remains a detached observer:

> On that day the city lets down its tumultuous hair, which the high summer anoints with warmth and perfume. In Paris every man has his girl; but on that day every man is a sultan. . . . No one is left outside; until the whole city has turned into one enormous party. To be alone in such a carnival is a strange experience. (p. 204)

For Jake, Paris is a city full of bittersweet memories of lost love (a relationship with Anna Quentin which also failed to develop in London), but he does rediscover artistic truth, and his existential ties demand solitude.

The inability to communicate which Donaghue experiences in Paris exemplifies one of the debates of linguistic analysis and is a major theme in the novel.[3] Hugo Belfounder, a Wittgenstein figure, views language as a limitation for truth. In a conversation with Jake, Hugo purposes that language precludes accuracy:

> "But suppose I try hard to be accurate," I said. "One can't be," said Hugo. "The only hope is to avoid say-

ing it. As soon as I start to describe, I'm done for. Try describing anything—our conversation, for instance—and you see how absolutely instinctively you—.''
''Touch it up?'' I suggested. ''It's deeper than that,'' said Hugo. ''The language just won't let you present it as it really was. . . . The whole language is a machine for making falsehoods.'' (p. 61–62)

Throughout *Under the Net* Murdoch juxtaposes the ''dignity of silence'' with the ''vulgarity of speech'' (p. 155) and thematically stresses the purity of silence. As narrator, Jake Donaghue records his conversations with Hugo in the form of a dialectic in which Annandine (Hugo) tells Tamarus (Jake) that ''only the greatest men can speak and still be truthful. . . . For most of us, for almost all of us, truth can be attained, if at all, only in silence'' (p. 88). This dialectic, following a classical Greek questioning method which is designed to discover truth, recreates conversations which Jake and Hugo had had while at a cold cure clinic. Jake originally wrote their conversations down as a dramatic exercise but came to view them as a possibility for legitimate publication (in comparison to his hack translating). But Jake's book, *The Silencer*, only proves Hugo's point concerning the average person's ability to tell the truth; it soon becomes ''a travesty and falsification'' of the conversations (p. 65). Donaghue even rationalizes his embellishment of the truth: ''Some of the most illuminating moments of our talk had been those which, if recorded, would have sounded the flattest. But these I never could bring myself to record with the starkness which they had had in reality'' (p. 65).

Because he feels he has misrepresented and betrayed Hugo, Jake is afraid to face him when *The Silencer* is published, so Jake skips an appointment with Hugo and then moves without leaving a forwarding address. Jake had valued Hugo's good opinion and eagerly anticipated their conversations; his betrayal, therefore, costs him a great deal of anxiety. Ironically, when the men meet again years later, Hugo discloses that he had been rather touched by Jake's book.

Anna Quentin also believes Hugo's ideas concerning silence and simple speech; following her association with Hugo, Anna relinquishes her singing career and concentrates her energies on a mime theater. Lozemnikov's farce *Marishka* is playing there, with Hugo acting the part of a burly simpleton being mocked by the other players (pp. 36–37), when Jake turns up at the theater looking for a place to stay. During the performance Anna talks to Jake about mime, equating its silence with both love (p. 41) and truth: "[Mime] is pure art. . . . It's very simple and it's very pure" (p. 42). And she adds, "only very simple things can be said without falsehood" (p. 44). For Anna, singing falls in the same category as speech, as a form of corruption (p. 44). Although Jake is upset with Anna for not continuing her singing career, she explains: " 'The sort of singing I do is so'—she searched for the word—'ostentatious. There's no truth in it. One's just exploiting one's charm to seduce people' " (p. 42).

Although Murdoch develops only five characters who are good people in twenty-four novels,[4] she does provide the reader with intimations of the good by presenting several underdeveloped characters who further clarify her beliefs on perfection, including Mrs. Tinckham from *Under the Net*. An "earth-goddess" and "aged Circe" (pp. 14, 277), Mrs. Tinckham keeps a "dusty, dirty, [and] nasty looking (p. 12) magazine shop which abounds in tabby cats. Jake Donaghue reports that "her shop serves as what is known as an 'accomodation address', and is a rendezvous for people who like to be very secretive about their affairs" (p. 14). She takes him into her shop when he is homeless and acts as a sounding board for his new discoveries about the complexities of life and love.

The descriptive "earth-goddess" identification relates to the unity characteristic of the good character, and Jake elaborates on the other attributes which she possesses: kindness, reliability, and discreetness. "She has been very kind to me, and I never forget kindness" (p. 14). The reader also learns that people confide in her and that she can keep a confidence:

The police have long ago given up questioning Mrs. Tinckham. It was time lost. However much or little she knows, she has never, in my experience, displayed either for profit or for effect any detailed acquaintance with the little world that circulates round her shop. . . . In the lives of many of her customers she probably figures as the only completely trustworthy confidant. (p. 15)

Much to Jake's embarrassment, when he finds out that his friend and valet, Finn, has returned to Ireland he also finds out that Finn had been thinking about going home for some time and had told Mrs. Tinckham about it, while Jake knew nothing of Finn's plans:

> The notion that Finn had made a confidante of Mrs.
> Tinckham came to me for the first time and rushed in
> an instant from possibility to probability. "He told you
> just before he went?" I asked. "Yes," said Mrs.
> Tinckham, "and earlier too. But he must have told
> you he wanted to go back?" "He did, now I come to
> think of it," I said, "but I didn't believe him. . . ." I
> felt ashamed, ashamed of being parted from Finn, of
> having known so little about Finn, of having conceived
> things as I pleased and not as they were. (p. 272)

Here Jake's narrow perception of otherness contrasts with the characteristics of the good which Mrs. Tinckham displays.

Hugo Belfounder also exemplifies the good. He imparts truth, even though he is not thoroughly aware of it, and is the Murdoch spokesman who marks the correlation between truth and beauty in the novel. Hugo has long dialectics with Jake on the subject of truth, but Hugo does not entirely understand his statements, for when they are embellished and published as *The Silencer,* Hugo admits that he found *The Silencer* "terribly hard in parts" (p. 240) and does not recognize the ideas as his own.

Hugo does, however, possess the general characteristics of the good character: recognition of others as separate from oneself, creativity, and selflessness. An ardent pacifist, he turned the flourishing armaments factory left to him by his father into a rocket (fireworks) factory (pp. 55–56). He became a highly skilled and creative craftsman at his own factory, specializing in set pieces. And, according to Jake, "Hugo treated the set piece as if it were a symphony" (p. 56). Other tributes to Hugo's goodness include his descriptions as an "idealist," a "purely objective and detached person" (p. 59) and "an almost completely truthful man" of "spiritual worth" (p. 64).

Philosophically, Hugo holds "no general theories whatsoever" (p. 61) and is reportedly responsible for such aphorisms as "the movement away from theory and generality is the movement towards truth" (p. 87) and "actions don't lie, words always do" (p. 250). While arguably unaware of his talents, Hugo extensively proselytizes Murdoch's moral philosophy and aesthetics and impresses his ideas on his fellow characters, for they mimic his beliefs—Jake writes *The Silencer* and Anna Quentin begins a mime theater. Because Murdoch meant *Under the Net* to be an existential novel, Hugo is a man of action and must be judged by his actions. He changes the munitions factory into a rocket factory, sells the rocket factory because he does not believe in private enterprise (p. 243), gives his money to the Socialist cause, and becomes apprenticed to a watchmaker in Nottingham (p. 250). These actions, finally, indicate his moral worth.

### *The Bell* (1958)

"With *The Bell* [Iris] Murdoch emerges as the best of the young novelists,"[5] said one critic. She does so with veracity of character and well-paced plot. The novel emphasizes the importance of living a spiritual life by learning to love others and explores this topic through various characters' interpretations of the ideal life.

Set in Gloucestershire, *The Bell* details the lives of members of a religious lay community attached to a cloistered Benedictine Anglican abbey. The members of Imber Court are brought together in their desire to live a contemplative life but ultimately are unable to sustain this utopian community. The community leader, Michael Meade, a failed priest, former schoolteacher, and chaste homosexual, cannot forgive himself for his past involvement with a former pupil, Nick Fawley, who lives in the lodge near Imber Court. And the presence of the emotionally unstable Nick, staying at the lodge to be near his twin sister, Catherine, who is planning to enter the Abbey as a postulant in the fall, serves as a constant reminder to Michael of his spiritual failures.

While the members' spiritual shortcomings may in themselves have led to the disintegration of the community, the introduction of two outsiders hastens its dissolution. Toby Gashe, a young Londoner, spends the summer before going up to Oxford with the community. And Dora Greenfield, a free spirit and stray wife, visits her husband, Paul, an art historian connected with the Courtauld Institute and studying medieval documents at the Abbey, while deciding if she will return to him.

Toby's role in the novel as catalyst is necessary but not as interesting as Dora's, for he lacks her spiritual growth. Toby's innocence is dispelled through his attachment both to Dora and to Michael Meade. Here he plays the double, repeating

### EARLY MAJOR WORKS (1954-1962)

the circumstances of Michael's earlier failings with Nick Farley; but Toby counters his fears of being homosexual in part by his secret plot with the bell and his courtly love of Dora. In a private sermon, Nick tells Toby that he has seen him tempting both Michael and Dora:

> "I've seen you at it," said Nick. "I've seen your love life in the woods, tempting our virtuous leader to sodomy and our delightful penitent to adultery. . . . I wonder if you have any idea of the harm you're causing? To poor Michael for instance. . . . You are busy destroying a man's faith, undermining his life, preparing his ruin—and even then you can't give it all your attention but start playing charades with a bloody bitch!"[6]

Toby's "charades" have a devastating effect on Michael and Nick, for following the sermon Nick sends Toby to confess to James Tayper Pace, and Nick then commits suicide while James is confronting Michael with Toby's confession (pp. 317, 321). Murdoch sends Toby back to London at the end of the summer, and he will go on to Oxford as a more serious and wiser youth.

Although initially insecure and dominated by her cold and authoritarian husband, Dora comes to self-knowledge and independence through her Imber experiences and is thereby saved from her aimless life. A free spirit, she lives in the present and has difficulty judging between right and wrong (p. 202). Members of the community view Paul as a wronged husband, and Dora often felt "that the community were easily, casually even, judging her, placing her'' (p. 141). Yet Dora is capable of unconscious acts of virtue: even though she is a nonswimmer, she follows Catherine into the lake to prevent her from suicide (p. 300); earlier she had rescued a Red Admiral butterfly from the train (p. 21).

Like many other Murdoch characters who gain insight about their lives through epiphanies, Dora eventually realizes her selfishness and muddle. She left the community and returned to London to contemplate her future, but while at the National Gallery gazing at Gainsborough's painting of his two daughters, she realized that her real life and problems were at Imber and that she must return there in order to face them:

> Dora was always moved by the pictures. Today she was moved, but in a new way. She marvelled, with a kind of gratitude, that they were all still here, and her heart was filled with love for the pictures, their authority, their marvellous generosity, their splendour. It occurred to her that here at last was something real and something perfect. Who had said that about perfection and reality being in the same place? . . . But the pictures were something real outside herself, which spoke to her kindly and yet in sovereign tones, something superior and good whose presence destroyed the dreary trance-like solipsism of her earlier mood (pp. 203, 204).

Good art, for Iris Murdoch, can bring one outside oneself and expose truths about the world. Dora's mystical experience in the National Gallery alerts her to the way out of her muddled existence. Unlike many of the enlightened characters from other Murdoch novels (for example, Effingham Cooper in *The Unicorn*) who lack the will to lead the difficult, more truthful life revealed by their epiphanies, Dora returns to Imber, forces herself to become responsible and independent, and eventually returns to painting.

The central symbol in the novel, the abbey's bell, is also the focus of the plot. At the end of the summer the lay community will replace the missing bell, Gabriel, which may have been thrown into the lake at the time of the dissolution of the monasteries. Another explanation for its disappearance is a legend which states that sometime during the fourteenth century the bell "flew like a bird out of the tower and fell into the lake" when a nun accused of having a lover refused to confess (p. 42). When Toby discovers the medieval bell while diving in the lake, he shares his secret with Dora; they plan to surprise the community by substituting the original bell for the new one at the ceremony in which the new bell is to be taken into the abbey. Although both are not innocent in their intentions, Toby viewing the bell as a quest and proof of his love for Dora (p. 231) and Dora wanting to play the witch in the community (p. 213), they are unaware of the tragic consequences which their stunt will have: Nick's suicide, Catherine's attempted suicide and mental breakdown, public notoriety for the community, and the dissolution of the community.

Murdoch's description of the mechanics involved in the raising of the bell, the substitution of the medieval bell for the new bell, and the medieval bell's mysterious tumbling through the causeway and into the lake while being taken to the abbey are vivid, realistic, and plausible. Her gift for mechanical descriptions is used in several later novels.[7]

The inscription on the medieval bell, "*Vox ego sum Amoris. Gabriel vocor.* I am the voice of Love. I am called Gabriel" (p. 237), recalls the central theme of the novel; the members of Imber Court have difficulty maintaining love for one another because they are too concerned with the external measurements of a moral life: rules, order, and judgment. The new bell shares part of this inscription: "Upon the shoulder of the bell there was also written, and it gave Dora a curious feeling to see it, *Gabriel vocor*" (p. 258).

The main question of the novel, how one should best live as a spiritual being, is answered ineffectively in sermons given by Michael Meade and James Tayper Pace, who, in keeping with their personalities and spiritual failures, provide contrasting answers. James, previously an Anglican social worker in the East End of London, came to Imber Court when his health failed because of overwork (p. 88). Many members of the community recognize him as the natural leader, and Michael describes him as "a man of more confident faith and more orthodox and rigid moral conceptions" than himself (p. 90). Peter Conradi notes that James is "one to whom ethics is a matter of unthinking rules and duties,"[8] and James makes this clear in his sermon: "The chief requirement of the good life . . . is to live without any image of oneself" (p. 138). He believes in rules, not ideals: " 'The good man *does* what seems right, what the rule enjoins, without considering the consequences, without calculation or prevarication, *knowing* that God will make all for the best. He does not amend the rules by the standards of this world' (p. 139).

Michael, less self-assured than James, finds leadership awkward; he feels judged by James "as a man with 'ideals but no principles' " (p. 90). Because "Michael had always held the view that the good man is without power" (p. 89), his sermon urges respect for human differentiation: "The chief requirement of the good life . . . is that one should have some conception of one's capacities. . . . One must study carefully how best to use such strength as one has" (p. 214). Unlike James, Michael feels that "one must perform the lower act which one can manage and sustain, not the higher act which one bungles" (p. 215). "As spiritual beings, in our imperfection and also in the possibility of our perfection, we differ profoundly one from another" (p. 218). Michael's sermon commends what James had called the second best act: "the act which goes with exploring one's personality and estimating the consequences rather than austerely following the rules" (p. 220).

Both men also use images of the bell in their sermons. While James imagines the bell sings out in innocence and truth (p. 143), Michael says, "The bell is subject to the force of gravity. The swing that takes it down must also take it up. So we too must learn to understand the mechanism of our spiritual energy, and find out where, for us, are the hiding places of our strength" (p. 219).

By presenting extremes, both sermons provide inadequate views of the good life. Murdoch establishes a far more tolerant view of human behavior with her development of the Abbess's advice to learn to love one another.[9] Although removed from the world, the Abbess gives a balanced view of goodness when she refers to love:

> "Often we do not achieve for others the good that we intend; but we achieve something, something that goes from our effort. Good is an overflow. . . . We can only learn to love by loving. Remember that all our failures are ultimately failures in love. Imperfect love must not be condemned and rejected, but made perfect." (p. 253)

The Abbess's realistic advice shows recognition of the tribulations connected with striving toward the good.

Although the lay community has not been a success, some of its members have learned to accept their spiritual inadequacies, recognize the difficulty of living a spiritual life, and think of others. Michael Meade realizes that his imperfect spirituality was responsible for Nick's death:

> He remembered now when it was useless how the Abbess had told him that the way was always forward. Nick had needed love, and he ought to have given him what he had to offer, without fears about its imperfection. If he had had more faith he would have done so, not calculating either Nick's faults or his own. (p. 332–33)

Now that Nick is dead and Nick's twin sister, Catherine, is in a mental institution,[10] Michael recognizes his continuing responsibility to her: He "knew in a cold sad way that till the end of his life he would be concerned with her and responsible for her welfare. Nick was gone; and to perfect his suffering Catherine remained" (p. 333).

### *An Unofficial Rose* (1962)

*An Unofficial Rose* opens with the funeral of Fanny Peronett. At her burial, Fanny's husband of more than forty years, Hugh, catches sight of the great love of his youth, Emma Sands, for whom he had failed to leave his wife. Hugh hopes to rekindle that romance, but Emma, now a popular detective writer of trite trash (as evidenced by an excerpt from one of her novels), has other plans. She wants to meet and manipulate Hugh's children and grandchildren but is not romantically interested in Hugh.

The iconography, an important element in Murdoch's novels, revolves around a Tintoretto nude, described as "an earlier version of the figure of Susannah in the great Susannah Bathing in Vienna. . . . It was a picture which might well enslave a man, a picture round which crimes might be committed."[11] Hugh reveals that he may have married Fanny because he coveted the painting, and their son, Randall, now expects his father to sell the Tintoretto to finance his liaison with Lindsey Rimmer, a secretary-companion to Emma Sands, primarily because Hugh had lacked the courage for a similar action during his youth. This Shakespearean doubling of circumstances (here taking place one generation later, with

Randall actually leaving his wife) is a recurring motif in Murdoch's later fiction. In this novel, the shared circumstance becomes the means by which the son bullies his father into an almost vicarious participation in his affair: "Randall the child had suffered from his father's temporary unfaithfulness; Randall the man must have meditated on the significance of his father's ultimate faithfulness. And it came to Hugh in a moment: he stands now where I stood then" (p. 175).

One could argue that in their concerns for freedom and action, Murdoch's characters are still existential, but as Peter Conradi points out in *Iris Murdoch: The Saint and the Artist,* many of the characters discover that their actions are not their own, that they were in part engineered by others.[12] For example, Hugh sells his beloved Tintoretto when his son repeats the situation of his youth. Hugh even thinks he has set Randall free: "It had been his own private *coup,* his own privately arranged alteration of the face of the world, the beautiful, extravagant, feckless setting of Randall free" (pp. 341–342). Yet Randall worries that Emma had made him fall in love with Lindsay: "He had loved Lindsay as the enticing but untouchable *princesse lointaine* which Emma had (how deliberately and with what end?) made of her . . ." (p. 310). And Randall's wife, Ann, who is loved by Felix Meecham, discovers after she has refused Felix's proposal that her action has been influenced by the manipulation of her daughter, Miranda, who is in love with Felix herself: "So the act had been Miranda's, it had indeed all happened 'on another plane.' She had had no act at all of her own, she had been part of someone else's scheme . . ." (p. 335). The characters are often unaware that their actions have been influenced by others: Hugh leaves for

### EARLY MAJOR WORKS (1954-1962)

India at the close of the novel, accompanied by Mildred and Humphrey Finch. Reflecting on recent events, Hugh thinks: "Perhaps he . . . had understood nothing, but he had certainly survived. He was free" (p. 344). He is unaware that the voyage has long been planned by Mildred, who has loved him for years.

The creative energies of Randall, a horticulturalist, have established the Peronett rose nursery: "It was his patient work which had produced the series of new roses, most of them now well known, by which the name of Peronett would be remembered" (p. 21). Perhaps the least attractive character in the novel, Randall is a failed artist who has never grown up. Described as "certainly a Peter Pan" (p. 18), an often used image for selfish and childish characters who fail to accept adult responsibilities, Randall maintains an attachment to his childhood toys and feels he is somehow pursuing a quest in Lindsay (pp. 72, 199). Through the course of the novel, however, he does come to recognize his limitations in an epiphany:

He knew in his heart, and he knew that Lindsay assumed, that he would never be a playwright. Distanced now by so much more of experience and suffering from his plays he realised clearly that they were no good. They were pretentious, muddled and insipid. . . . There was only one thing in the world that he was really good at [horticulture], and that he would never do again. . . . (p. 312)

In keeping with her belief that "a cat can love a king," Murdoch presents complex romantic entanglements. Randall Peronett loves his wife, Ann and his mistress, Lindsey Rimmer; he is loved by these women, the servant girl Nancy Bow-shott and Emma Sands. Emma is attached to Hugh, Penn, Lindsey, and Jocelyn, among others. This courtly dance of changing partners is a common but often surprising plot mechanism in Murdoch's novels. The duplicating plot mechanism involving the father and son also has a reversal with Hugh's taking Randall's place as Emma's chaperon when Randall elopes with Lindsey Rimmer (p. 323).

Emma Sands, one of Murdoch's mesmerizing figures, has something attractive about her and also something which is wicked. When Randall visits her he lays "the roses down on the little table with a gesture of donation" (p. 200). And he thinks, "She has brought me here, she has drawn me here, witch-like, out of London, it is she who has summoned me" (p. 201). In addition, "Emma had always seemed to [Felix] an exotic and slightly dangerous figure" (p. 158). Emma had loved Felix when he was fourteen (p. 321), and she is attracted to both sprite-like girls and young boys who have "that particular faun-like grace which fades later" (p. 321).

One remarkable character in the novel, Ann Peronett, has several characteristics of the good but finally fails in terms of knowledge, awareness, and awareness of others. She is perceived as a "*good* person" with unreflective Christian piety by her father-in-law, Hugh (p. 183), and as "good . . . [unable to] be bad," by her very conventional admirer, Colonel Felix Meecham (p. 297), who also perceives her as "the ideal English woman" (p. 159) to whom he plays the courtly lover. Her husband, Randall, views Ann as unselfish. Her behavior in his regard proves she possesses the humility and denigration of self required for perfection, for Randall is having an affair and wants not only his freedom but also the assurance that Ann will maintain their home for his possible later return. Felix, who had admired Ann for years, views Randall's departure as the opportunity to pursue his chances with her. Ann loves Felix ''dreadfully'' (p. 265) but eventually sends him away, deciding to wait for Randall: '' 'Perhaps I've forgotten how [to do what I want],' she said slowly. 'I don't in a way see myself. I see him. It's not that I'm being unselfish. He just too much *is*' '' (p. 297).

Elizabeth Dipple, among other critics, places Ann at the highest level of good, but she also recognizes the fault which precludes this tribute, Ann's lack of awareness, and calls Ann an ''unconsciously good character.''[13] This state is revealed by Ann's actions and by her conversation with another admirerer, the Reverend Douglas Swann. Ann states that she has ''lived in unconsciousness too long,'' and the Reverend Swann, identified earlier as ''not impeccably wise'' (p. 268), replies that ''being good is a state of unconsciousness'' (p. 270). Whatever the merits of Swann's belief, Ann's lack of vision results in her indecisive action and faulty communication. She decides to stay and wait for Randall's return primarily because his presence is larger than her own, and she sends Felix away without actually intending to do so: ''Looking back on her last interview with Felix, Ann felt that it had simply been a muddle'' (p. 328). She really did not want to sever the connection between them, ''only it was too late. She had not meant the words as Felix had taken them. She had only meant . . . to show him everything, the ultimate difficulties. . . . But the picture, as she had too truthfully revealed it, was too much for him'' (p. 329).

Ann's behavior cannot be construed as altogether harmless. A married woman, she willingly maintains close friendships with two men who have more than a friendly interest in her, Douglas Swann (himself a married priest) and Felix Meecham, and she takes advantage of their feelings when she is deserted by Randall and requires attention from Felix and advice about Felix from Swann. Also, in part she encourages Randall's childish and egoistic behavior by allowing him to disregard their marriage vows with impunity. And since she is unaware of Miranda's secret love for Felix, Ann cannot communicate with her daughter once Miranda percieves Ann's interest in him, nor can she discover how to reestablish relations with Miranda once Felix leaves. Finally, Ann's Australian nephew, Penn Graham, is made miserable by his separateness from and neglect by the Peronett household and particularly by Miranda's taunting him about his foreign mannerisms. Ann could certainly have made Penn more at ease with her family during his visit had she not been so preoccupied with her own troubles. Therefore, Ann fails to qualify as a good character on the grounds of knowledge, vision, and consciousness of others.

## Notes

1. "Closing Debate," in *Rencontres avec Iris Murdoch*, ed. Jean-Louis Chevalier (Caen: Centre de Recherches de Littérature et Linguistique des Pays

## EARLY MAJOR WORKS (1954-1962)

de Langue Anglaise, 1978), p. 76. Iris Murdoch says, "*Under the Net . . .* was much influenced by Samuel Beckett and Raymond Queneau, though I don't think it particularly resembles anything by either of them, but that wasn't my fault, I was copying them as hard as I could!"

2. Iris Murdoch, *Under the Net* (New York: Viking, 1954), p. 104; subsequent references to this work are noted parenthetically in the text. For further London associations, see Louis L. Martz, "Iris Murdoch: The London Novels," in *Twentieth Century Literature in Retrospect,* ed. Reuben A. Brower (Cambridge: Harvard University Press, 1971), pp. 65–86.

3. The dominant philosophical school at Oxford when Iris Murdoch taught philosophy there was linguistic analysis, but Murdoch is interested in moral philosophy.

4. See the discussion of "good" in the introductory chapter.

5. William Van O'Connor, "Iris Murdoch: The Formal and the Contingent," *Critique* 3, no. 2 (1960): 34–46.

6. Iris Murdoch, *The Bell* (New York: Viking, 1958), pp. 279–80 subsequent references to this work are noted parenthetically in the text.

7. See, for example, the car accident in *The Book and the Brotherhood.*

8. Peter Conradi, *Iris Murdoch: The Saint and the Artist* (New York: St. Martin's Press, 1986), p. 116.

9. Conradi's work (pp. 116–18) has an excellent discussion of the partial views of good presented in both sermons and the balanced view presented by the Abbess.

10. When the bell fell into the lake, Catherine, who secretly loved Michael Meade, had a mental and physical collapse and attempted suicide. She felt that the loss of the bell was a sign of her unworthiness for the convent.

11. Iris Murdoch, *An Unofficial Rose* (New York: Viking, 1962), pp. 92–93; subsequent references to this work are noted parenthetically in the text.

12. Conradi, p. 60.

13. Elizabeth Dipple, *Iris Murdoch: Work for the Spirit* (Chicago: University of Chicago Press, 1982), p. 19.

# CHAPTER FOUR

# Major Works of the Middle Period (1968–1973)

### *The Nice and the Good* (1968)

Iris Murdoch's titles reflect the meaning of her novels, and the title of this novel is no exception. Typical of the multilayered texture of her work. *The Nice and the Good* successfully integrates her moral philosophy, aesthetics, and characterization. Nice and good, levels of awareness and correct action in Murdoch's moral philosophy, are distinguished in the novel through characterization. Although there are no good characters in the novel, two characters, John Ducane and Theodore Gray, have intimations of the good, and Theo recognizes the vast disparity between the spiritual states indicated by the novel's title.

The main settings of the novel include a Whitehall department in London and the Dorset seaside estate to which this department's head, Octavian Gray, and his fellow civil servant, John Ducane, retreat on weekends. The major themes in the novel emerge as these men's Whitehall concerns also mix with family and friends at Trescombe House and Trescombe Cottage in Dorset. Sacred and profane love, the seductive nature of power and the evil which it produces, justice, and forgiveness concern the novel's characters in their efforts to achieve good lives.

Initially, Ducane, the legal representative of the Whitehall department headed by Octavian Gray, and Theodore Gray, Octavian's elder brother living at Trescombe House, appear as unlikely fellow spokesmen of the good. Ducane, the central character in the novel, comes to recognize, through a near-death experience, the true nature of power and the dreariness of evil. By contrast, the innocuous and almost invisible Uncle Theo has already experienced the "gulf" which separates him from the good and has been broken by his dispair of ever becoming good. Both men are necessary for the explanation of the nearly unattainable good in Murdoch's moral philosophy; Ducane will return to the everyday world with enhanced spiritual awareness, but Uncle Theo will attempt real spiritual purification by returning to his Buddhist monastery without the consolations provided by the world.

An expert on Roman law whose ambition is "to lead a clean simple life and to be a good man,"[1] Ducane appears an upright example of justice. But when asked to investigate the suicide of a Whitehall civil servant, Joseph Radeechy, he finds himself caught up in a moral muddle. Although he aspires to be "the just man and the just judge" (p. 77), Ducane is repulsed by his discovery that Radeechy's private life included a considerable interest in the occult and the performance of black masses in the Whitehall vaults (complete with pigeon sacrifices and a naked woman in attendance). Furthermore, Ducane finds himself attracted to Judy McGrath (also known as Helen of Troy), the same woman whom Radeechy had used for his black masses. Ducane's private life is also morally questionable, for he has been trying to free himself of his former mistress, Jessica Bird, so that he might engage (with clear conscience) in a harmless flirtation with his Whitehall superior's wife, Kate Gray. He also worries about his satisfaction over being in the position of power over another Whitehall employee whom he dislikes when Richard Biranne is implicated in Radeechy's affairs.

However, Ducane remains a spokesman for the good because he recognizes the evil in his own life: "I am the perfect whited sepulchre, Ducane thought. I've fiddled and compromised with two women and been a failure with one and a catastrophe to the other. . . . I cannot feel compassion for those over whom I imagine myself to be set as a judge" (p. 271). And he correctly assesses the childish nature of Radeechy's darker powers:

> It's the dreariness of it, thought Ducane, that stupefies. This evil is dreary, it's something shut in and small, dust falling upon cobwebs, a blood-stain upon a garment, a heap of dead birds in a packing-case. Whatever it was that Radeechy had so assiduously courted and attracted to himself and which had breathed upon him, squirted over him, that odour of decay, had no intensity or grandeur. These were but small powers, graceless and bedraggled. (pp. 230–31)

As Ducane's position of power becomes uncomfortable, he feels unworthy and finds it increasingly difficult to be another man's judge (p. 271).

## MAJOR WORKS OF THE MIDDLE PERIOD (1968–1973)

Ducane's epiphany, following the near-death experience of being trapped in Gunnar's cave while the sea waters rise around him, illuminates the truly important things in life:

> If I ever get out of here I will be no man's judge. Nothing is worth doing except to kill the little rat [ego], not to judge, not to be superior, not to exercise power, not to seek, seek, seek. To love and to reconcile and to forgive, only this matters. All power is sin and all law is frailty. Love is the only justice. Forgiveness, reconciliation, not law. (p. 329)

Few characters who experience such vision are able to sustain it by changing their lives for the better. Following his epiphany, Ducane returns Radeechy's confession to Biranne and asks Biranne to try to reconcile with his wife. Receiving letters of release and dismissal from both Jessica and Kate, Ducane marries Mary Clothier—they had been attracted to the good in one another. He resigns his civil-service position and plans to go into teaching and research.

It is for Theo Gray to establish the distance which separates the nice from the good and to show the necessity of forgiveness, even of oneself. Theo, overtly a cranky old man, hardly counts as a man at Trescombe House (p. 18), and, like many of Murdoch's saintly characters, he appears almost invisible. Beneath his crusty surface, however, Theo struggles to control his carnal urges towards the young Pierce Clothier and gives helpful and morally good advice to the residents of Trescombe House and to Willy Kost, an emotionally maimed Jewish refugee living in Trescombe Cottage.

### UNDERSTANDING IRIS MURDOCH

Both Theo and Willy have past transgressions for which they cannot forgive themselves, and their despair affects their spiritual growth. Willy suffers from melancholia, thought to be a result of his experiences in Dachau; ironically, this melancholia does not result from what the Nazis did to him but from his betrayal of two people who died as a result of his cowardice. Theo's dark past concerns something that happened in Delhi. While in India Theo had taken vows in a Buddhist monastery, but he left after an incident with a young novice who later was drowned in the Ganges (p. 374). Since then Theo has lived as a recluse on his brother's estate. His sister-in-law, Kate, calls him "a broken reed, a bundle of nerves" (p. 47), and he appears to Mary Clothier "as a man who had been through the inferno and had by the experience been deprived of his will" (p. 90).

Although unable to forgive himself for his own actions, Willy recognizes a fellow sufferer in Theo and gives him this advice: "I can forgive you, Theo. I can't absolve you. You must absolve yourself. Pardon the past and let it go . . . absolutely . . . away" (p. 134). Theo cannot apply his knowledge in his own life, but he too understands the importance of forgiving oneself and focusing on the good. When Willy finally confesses his guilt to Theo, Theo thinks,

What can I say to him? That one must soon forget
one's sins in the claims of others. But how to forget.
The point is that nothing matters except loving what is
good. Not to look at evil but to look at good. Only
this contemplation breaks the tyranny of the past,

breaks the adherence of evil to the personality, breaks,
in the end, the personality itself. In the light of the
good, evil can be seen in its place, not owned, just
existing, in its place. Could he explain all this to
Willy? He would have to try. (p. 371)

Theo's actions ultimately distinguish him from Willy and
Ducane, both of whom have some knowledge and pursuit of
the truth. After he left the Buddhist monastery, Theo continued to cling to the notion that his Buddhist mentor could help
him find peace, and this consolation is one of Theo's minor
faults. The action which indicates his spiritual progression is
his decision to return to India following his mentor's death. In
fact, Theo's spiritual maturation can be measured by the pro-
cesses by which he initially joins the monastery, decides to
leave it, and finally realizes that he must return. The first days
of Theo's novitiate reveal naiveté: "He had seemed to leave
his past utterly behind when, with a passion which seemed a
guarantee of renewed life, he had entered into the community
of these men" (p. 375). But he found that even in the monastery perfection was not so easily obtained: "To find himself
even there the same being as before shocked his pride, the re-
lentless egoism which he now saw had not suffered an iota of
dimunition from his gesture of giving up the world" (p. 375).
And Theo is shaken by his glimpse of the notion of what being
good actually entails:

Theo had begun to glimpse the distance which separates the nice from the good, and the vision of this
gap had terrified his soul. He had seen, far off, what

> is perhaps the most dreadful thing in the world, the
> other face of love, its blank face. Everything that he
> was, even the best that he was, was connected with
> possessive self-filling human love. That blank demand
> implied the death of his whole being. (p. 375)

Clearly not ready to face the mental rigors of perfection, Theo
turns to another consolation: "Perhaps it was to calm the
frenzy of this fear that he had so much and so suddenly needed
to hold tightly in his arms a beautiful golden-skinned boy"
(p. 375).

The realization that he lacks the mental discipline to face
the good alone causes Theo to leave the monastery and return
to England, where he clings to one final consolation, depen-
dence on his mentor. He believes that as long as his mentor
lives, the opportunity to try again will remain open for him.
But once he learns that the old man has died, Theo rationalizes that the optimum moment has passed and that it is too late
for him to return to the monastery (p. 376). Yet Theo also has
the vision to realize that it is for this very reason that he should
at last return: "The old man would have understood this, the
action without fruits. . . . Although he might never draw a
single step closer to that great blankness, he would know of its
reality and feel more purely in the simplicity of his life the dis-
tant plucking of its magnetic power" (pp. 376–77). Theo's decision to return without consolation, to be good for nothing,
indicates his spiritual maturity and places him as one of Murdoch's nearly good figures.

The iconography for the novel is taken from Agnolo
Bronzino's *An Allegory*. A watercolor sketch of the painting

## MAJOR WORKS OF THE MIDDLE PERIOD (1968–1973)

dominates the cover of the Chatto & Windus first edition, and a detail from it is photographically reproduced on the cover of the current Penguin paperback edition of the novel. Although all of the characters in the novel can identify with the painting, Richard and Paula Biranne are most closely associated with it:

> It was long ago, before their marriage even, that Richard had "taken over" that picture of Bronzino's. It was he who had first made her really *look* at it, and it had become the symbol of their courtship, a symbol which Paula had endorsed the more since she found it in a way alien to her. It was a transfiguration of Richard's sensuality, Richard's lechery, and she took it to her with a quick gasp of surprise even as she took Richard. (pp. 150–51)

Murdoch provides a detailed description of Bronzino's painting during one of Paula's visits to the National Gallery:

> Paula sat and looked at the picture. A slim elongated naked Venus turns languidly towards a slim elongated naked Cupid. Cupid stoops against her, his long-fingered left hand supporting her head, his long-fingered right hand curled about her left breast. His lips have just come to rest very lightly upon hers, or perhaps just beside hers. It is the long still moment of dreamy suspended passion before the spinning clutching descent. Against a background of smooth masks and desperate faces the curly-headed Folly advanced to deluge with rose petals the drugged and amorous pair,

> while the old lecher Time himself reaches out a long
> and powerful arm above the scene to bring all sweet
> things to an end. (p. 151)

Here the emphasis is on the erotic kiss, for the central attraction between the Birannes had been sexual. But following
their divorce, when Paula contemplates reuniting with Richard, she notices a different part of the painting: "Paula stared
at the enamel-faced figure of Deceit, and at her reversed hands
and scaly tail. Was it here, after all, that everything broke
down and descended into a roaring shaft of shattered masks
and crumpled rose petals and bloody feathers?" (pp. 351–52).
When she agrees to take Richard back, Paula tells him,
"All right. But lies do corrupt and spoil" (p. 352). And Richard, recognizing his inability to remain faithful indefinitely,
responds, "I know that. I would keep them to a minimum"
(p. 352).

   The interpretation of the allegory often varies, but
Homan Potterton provides the following explication:

> Cupid is indeed beguilded by the kiss of his mother
> Venus as she seeks to equip herself with his powers by
> robbing the arrow from his quiver. Jealousy tears her
> hair in anguish, while the head above her upon closer
> scrutiny is seen to be nothing more than a hollow
> mask and is therefore probably Fraud. The girl in the
> green dress, half animal, half human, is Pleasure, and
> proffering a honeycomb in one hand and the sting
> from her tail in the other, reminds us of the dual as-
> pect of her nature: the sweetness she brings may also

## MAJOR WORKS OF THE MIDDLE PERIOD (1968–1973)

> lead to pain. The *putto* who prepares to shower the
> couple with roses is Folly. The aged winged figure,
> top right, is Time, and just as Venus disarms Cupid,
> so too does Time (by reaching for her drapery) attempt
> to disarm Fraud.[2]

Murdoch incorporates jealousy, masks, deceit, eroticism, and
the various guises of love from the painting into the plot of her
novel. While the Birannes are most closely associated with the
painting, all of the characters love badly and present false images of themselves. In addition, Jessica Bird's reaction to John
Ducane's attempts to leave her recalls the anguish shown by
the figure of jealousy, and Willy Kost's lecture to her about the
poison of jealousy evokes the image of a serpent's tail and the
pain brought by Pleasure (or Deceit). Pleasure (or Deceit) is
also shown by the McGraths, with Judy acting as the honey-
comb to lure the men (Radeechy, Biranne, and Ducane), and
her husband, Peter, providing the "sting" of blackmail. Judy
McGrath even calls John Ducane "Mr Honey" and "Mr.
Honeyman" (p. 268).

### *A Fairly Honourable Defeat* (1970)

*A Fairly Honourable Defeat,* as the title suggests, concerns the struggle between good and evil which takes place
in everyday life. In an alternate allegorical reading of the
novel endorsed by Murdoch herself, this struggle also involves
spiritual beings. The novel's cast of characters, small by

Murdoch's normal standards, includes Hilda and Rupert Foster, a middle-aged, idealistic couple. Hilda performs good works and belongs to several charitable organizations; Rupert, a Sunday metaphysician and civil servant, has been writing a book about "real virtue and morals" for the past eight years. Hilda's sister, Morgan, a linguistic theorist who is estranged from her husband, social worker Tallis Browne, has been living in America with Julius King, a biochemist involved with developing nerve gas. The Fosters' son, Peter, an antisocial layabout, lives with Tallis and Tallis's father, Leonard. Rupert's younger brother, Simon, and his lover, Axel Nilsson, complete the family group.

In her discussion of good and evil in *A Fairly Honourable Defeat*, Diana Phillips claims that the novel "exemplifies the eternal struggles between the forces of light and darkness over the human soul."[3] Murdoch, commenting on this approach to the novel, agrees that the novel is ambiguous: "At one level it's a perfectly straight forward story about a decent chap and a rotter, and marital love and mistakes and confusion and so on. But there is also this aspect to it, that you've brought out very well."[4]

This struggle between good and evil takes place between several characters, but primarily between Tallis Browne, the figure of good who is one of Murdoch's rare saintly figures, and the figure of darkness, Julius King. Commenting on the religious allegory in the novel, Murdoch identifies Julius King with the "devil" and calls Tallis "not exactly a Christ-figure, I think, but what in the East would be called a 'high incarnation.' He is a good person who's turned up, as they perhaps do every now and then, in the world, but he is also a spiritual

## MAJOR WORKS OF THE MIDDLE PERIOD (1968–1973)

being.''[5] She explains that Leonard, ''if you want to carry the allegory a little bit further into a kind of absurdity, is God the Father. He's Tallis's father, and he's constantly making the remark: 'It all went wrong from the start.' ''[6] Other critics agree with Peter Conradi, who finds that ''Morgan represents the human soul over which the two spiritual magnates are battling.''[7]

Murdoch's characters are, for the most part, high-minded and well intentioned. Rupert had read philosophy at Oxford, and his book is about ''the relation of love to truth and justice.''[8] Hilda tells her sister, Morgan, that the real purpose of life is loving people (p. 48). While none of these ideas is contrary to Murdoch's moral philosophy, Julius King recognizes the Fosters as a bit too self-righteous and sets about proving his theory that ''every man loves himself so astronomically more than he loves his neighbour'' (p. 225).

Morgan's representation displays the darker side of the human soul. Unfaithful, self-indulgent, and not wanting to ''*bother* with other people'' (p. 299), Morgan makes her egoism evident. She also claims a spiritual connection with the devil figure, Julius, calling him her ''godfather'' (p. 204) and a ''*god*'' (p. 163). Axel calls her ''completely malevolent'' (p. 197), and indeed she makes a wager with Julius which is directed against him. When Julius claims that he can ''divide anybody from anybody'' (p. 225), Morgan bets him ten guineas that he can't. They fix on separating the homosexual couple Simon Foster and Axel Nilsson (p. 226).

Axel and Simon are also unusual in traditional literature in that they are sympathetically portrayed. Murdoch claims that one of the things she wanted to do in *A Fairly Honourable*

*Defeat* was to portray a happy homosexual relationship;[9] she has known many such couples and wanted to show this situation in her novels. Murdoch sensitively establishes Simon and Axel as a believable, worthy, and normal couple. Rupert tells his wife, "My dear Hilda, being homosexual doesn't determine a man's whole character any more than being heterosexual does!" (p. 8). And through his relationship with Axel, Simon came to view himself as normal: "He made Simon understand for the first time that it was perfectly *ordinary* to be homosexual. . . . He had never quite seen it as a fundamental and completely ordinary way of being a human being, which was how Axel saw it" (p. 29–30). Ultimately their love for each other allows them to survive the jealousy and doubt which Julius maliciously plants in their lives.

The marriage of Rupert and Hilda, however, ends tragically. Unknown to Morgan, Julius decided to double his entertainment by also detaching the Fosters. He explains his reason for doing so: "Rupert started to hold forth about goodness, and this sort of talk sickens me, as I expect it does you. And I couldn't help wondering how old Rupert would stand up to a real test and what all this high-minded muck would really amount to in practice" (p. 392–93). Julius had stumbled upon Rupert's love letters, written to Hilda when they were courting. Julius also had lover letters written to him by Morgan. He thought he would be able to make Rupert and Morgan fall in love with each other because of their egoism: "When it came to it, it was surprisingly easy. . . . There's hardly any deception, if you choose it carefully enough, with which people will not co-operate. Egoism moves them, fear moves them, and off

## MAJOR WORKS OF THE MIDDLE PERIOD (1968–1973)

they go'' (p. 394). When his plan worked, Julius had only to hint to Hilda that Morgan and Rupert were having an affair and then plant one of Morgan's letters in Rupert's desk. Julius does confess to Tallis that he feels bad about Hilda's pain, primarily because she is a selfless person: ''She is a very good-natured and kindly person who doesn't think too much about herself. She's not *interested* in herself, the way the others are'' (p. 396).

Though Julius is described by Murdoch as being, on a literal level, a ''rotter,'' he is one of the attractive power figures in the Murdoch canon. Peter Conradi points to the masterful characterization on Murdoch's part that develops him beyond a flat caricature of evil.[10] Instead, readers find him interesting and in some ways sympathetic. As a biochemist, Julius worked on nerve gas and ''a kind of anthrax which resists antibiotics'' (p. 4), and he quit this job because of boredom, not out of any sense of morality. He had had a two-year love affair with Morgan, and she had left her husband for him. But now he was tired of Morgan and wanted her out of his life. Readers know that Julius is Jewish but do not learn until late in the novel that he was in a concentration camp during the war. Conradi also points out the influence of Simone Weil's writing on Julius's character: ''Weil believes extreme affliction is passed on by all except the saintly.''[11] Julius cannot absorb his suffering and so passes it on to the others around him.

There are hints that Julius is other than a mere mortal: he is ritualistic (p. 85) and ''believes in the iron hand of destiny'' (p. 75). When Simon tells Julius that ''it was a *demon* thing'' to set up the meeting between Morgan and Rupert, Julius

## UNDERSTANDING IRIS MURDOCH

refers to them as puppets (p. 255). His relationship with the good figure, Tallis Browne, is interesting. Julius tells Tallis that he didn't recognize him at first and clearly talks to him as an equal. It is as though they had been struggling over the souls about them, and each had won to some extent—Simon and Axel reconcile, but Rupert becomes a casualty of Julius's hoax, drowned in his own swimming pool before he and Hilda can reconcile.

Tallis Browne, presented as a good and gentle being in *A Fairly Honourable Defeat,* displays both correct vision and right conduct, traits which Iris Murdoch associates with the good.[12] Perhaps Murdoch's most successful and sustained rendering of a good character, Tallis endures his wife's affair with Julius King; nurses his bitter and raging father, Leonard; shelters homeless refugees; and takes Hilda and Rupert Foster's deviant son off their hands. He teaches adult education, does social work, and gives lectures on the Trade Union Movement, the housing department, and the Labour party (pp. 14, 49).

Initially Tallis appears unattractive; his life is messy and unorganized and filled with the problems of others. He does, however, experience some unusual spiritual phenomena. He is referred to as fey (p. 54) and has dreams and visions concerning his dead twin sister. Though most believe that Tallis's sister died of polio at age fourteen, she was actually raped and killed by a sex maniac, and Tallis believes he has visitations from her from some other region (p. 200). The visitations are accompanied by ''familiar and wearying phenomena: the booming sound [and] the sense of imminent light which never

**MAJOR WORKS OF THE MIDDLE PERIOD (1968–1973)**

quite became light. . . . In a mechanical and repetitious way these sensations were accompanied by the idea of love'' (p. 199–200).

Unlike Julius, who cannot fail to pass his suffering on to others, Tallis suffers from the tragic death of his sister, keeping it to himself, and tries to spread love to others.[13] Tallis also emerges as the only character in the novel who has the vision to look beyond himself. His judgments are realistic and correct. He admits that Peter Foster's lodging with him has not rehabilitated the boy (a dropout, con artist, and thief) and correctly assesses Peter's need of psychiatric help (p. 171). When Hilda and Rupert then try to push Peter off on Morgan, Tallis advises Morgan against adding Peter to her collection of men: ''Don't mess around with Peter . . . unless you're really prepared to commit yourself to him in some serious and sensible sort of way. Peter needs permanencies'' (p. 204).

Tallis displays authorative and correct action during an incident in a Chinese restaurant when five ''burly youths of about eighteen'' bully a Jamaican diplomat by holding him down, smashing his face, and calling him names (pp. 230–31). When Simon tries to intercede, the thugs turn on him; then Axel tries to reason with the men but has no success. Julius only stands by, his ''eyes gleaming with pleasure'' (p. 232). But Tallis does react:

The next moment something happened very quickly. Tallis moved in from behind Julius and before anyone could shift or cry out he had struck the youth very

> hard across the side of the face. He struck him with
> the flat of his hand but with such violence that the
> boy staggered back against his companions and almost
> fell to the floor. (p. 232)

Although shaken by his violence, Tallis alone of all of the men
had ended the matter swiftly and capably.

### The Black Prince (1973)

Winner of the James Tait Black Memorial Prize for fiction and the most critically acclaimed of Iris Murdoch's novels, *The Black Prince* illustrates its author's literary and popular success. Here her trademarks—careful plotting, fully realized characterization, and attention to details—are joined with a murder mystery of sorts through postscripts which suggest various readings of the novel. Through this closely-structured device, Murdoch again relates the life of the artist whose work has been impacted by Eros.

*The Black Prince* opens following a scene of domestic violence; Arnold Baffin telephones his best friend, Bradley Pearson, to report that he has just murdered his wife with a blow from a fireplace poker. Baffin has not actually succeeded in murdering his wife, Rachel, and by the novel's ending Pearson will receive yet another phone call, this time from Rachel, claiming that she has just murdered her husband with this same fireplace poker. Pearson will rush over to his friends' home to help and console; shortly thereafter, Pearson himself

### MAJOR WORKS OF THE MIDDLE PERIOD (1968–1973)

will be convicted of the murder of Arnold Baffin. Postscripts by dramatis personae, including Pearson, Francis Marloe (a homosexual quack psychiatrist), the scorned wife, Julian Baffin (the Baffins' twenty-year-old daughter), and a P. Loxias (identified by Murdoch as the god Apollo), tease the reader with various rationales for Pearson's motives and actions. The careful reader, however, will recognize that the real murderer (the wife) has gotten away with her crime by framing Pearson for her husband's murder. This conclusion, never directly stated by the author, must be reached by considering a complex set of motives for the two main suspects, Rachel and Pearson. Jealousy and vindictiveness are possible on Rachel's part, for she is rejected by both Pearson, who then has an affair with her daughter, and her husband, who has a new mistress. Pearson may be jealous of Baffin's literary success and is certainly outraged when Baffin interferes with his affair with Julian.

Initially Murdoch intrigues her reader with an "Editor's Foreword" by one P. Loxias, who claims to have been responsible for the publication of Bradley Pearson's book, *The Black Prince—A Celebration of Love*. Murdoch provided a clue to Loxias's identity when she asked a friend to draw a head of the statue of Apollo at Olympia for the novel's jacket,[14] yet the details for press releases by her American publisher, Viking (available with the Murdoch manuscripts at the University of Iowa), make it clear that the name Apollo should not appear in conjunction with the name Loxias. As a result, many critics misread the title. "*The Black Prince*, of course is Apollo— most critics who reviewed the book in England didn't appear to realize this, even though there was a picture of Apollo on the front!'' she noted in a French interview.[15] Instead, critics identified Bradley Pearson, the novel's protagonist, with Hamlet (known as the black prince because he is often pictured in sable robes of mourning). Bradley gives Julian Baffin a *Hamlet* tutorial, a wonderful piece mixing brilliant criticism with a bizarre Freudian interpretation, and he is able to consummate their affair (described almost as a rape) only after she dresses up as Hamlet.[16]

Murdoch makes the connection between Loxias and Apollo: ''Apollo, [is] a murderer, a rapist, as is said in the novel when they're discussing who Mr. Loxias is, who killed a fellow musician in a horrible way, a great power figure, but not necessarily a good figure.''[17] As Peter Conradi points out, Apollo is named as Luxius and Lycean in Sophocles' *Oedipus Rex*.[18] Throughout classical literature Apollo has been linked with music and is known for ravishing women. Murdoch has long associated the destruction of the ego, or sublimation of self, with the artist's creativity. She reiterated this position by choosing Titian's *The Flaying of Marsyas* as the background painting for her own portrait which now hangs in the National Portrait Gallery. In Titian's painting, Apollo is seen as lovingly removing the satyr Marsyas' skin (following Marsyas' loss to Apollo in their famed music contest). The doubling of the Apollo-Marsyas myth is repeated in Pearson's supposed murder of his fellow-artist and friend, the popular novelist Arnold Baffin; his forceful consummation of his affair with Julian; and Pearson's own suffering and death as necessary for the production of his work of art, the novel *The Black Prince*.

## MAJOR WORKS OF THE MIDDLE PERIOD (1968–1973)

For Murdoch, Titian's painting of the Apollo-Marsyas myth conveys "something to do with human life and all its ambiguities and all its horrors and terrors and misery and at the same time there's something beautiful, the picture is beautiful, and something also to do with the entry of the spiritual into the human situation and the closeness of the gods."[19] And she has stated that she "regard[s] Dionysus in a sense as a part of Apollo's mind . . . and want[s] to exalt Apollo as a god who is a terrible god, but also a great artist and thinker and a great source of life."[20] Apollo has influenced Bradley Pearson's life: "Bradley is somehow destroyed by art; he's also destroyed by the black Eros, whom I identify in a way with Apollo. But the voice of Apollo is very much there—a cold, ambiguous voice.[21] These connotations, which recall the classical celebration of death in life, are illustrated iconographically not only in *The Black Prince* but also in *The Good Apprentice, A Fairly Honourable Defeat,* and *A Word Child.*

Bradley Pearson, the narrator of *The Black Prince,* is a fifty-eight-year-old civil servant with some limited literary publications who is taking an early retirement in order to satisfy a lifelong creative urge and write his "great work," which will be a commentary on art and love. Here Murdoch extends the French symbolist debate between Rimbaud and Mallarmé about how truth can be told. Should art be crystalline and compact or journalistic and loosely written?

*The Black Prince* presents two failed artists, one representing each style. Pearson has steadily destroyed most of what he has written through the years because his writing has failed to live up to his aesthetic standards; but his friend

## UNDERSTANDING IRIS MURDOCH

Arnold Baffin routinely churns out one success after another. The men frequently quarrel about their craft:

> "Art isn't chat plus fantasy. Art comes out of endless restraint and silence."
> "If the silence is endless there isn't any art! It's people without creative gifts who say that more means worse!"
> "One should only complete something when one feels one's bloody privileged to have it at all. Those who only do what's easy will never be rewarded by—"
> "Nonsense. I write whether I feel like it or not. I complete things whether I think they're perfect or not. Anything else is hypocrisy. I have no muse. That's what being a professional writer is."
> "Then thank God I'm not one."[22]

Not only does Murdoch present the reader with a clash of aesthetic opposites between two egoistic artists, but she also provides ample motives for murder and evidence of guilt. Looking back over the novel's events, the reader could piece together a plausible explanation for Pearson's conviction. Once a hysterical Rachel telephones Pearson, telling him that she has just murdered her husband, Pearson expects to find a scenario similar to that described in Arnold's first phone call. Instead he arrives to find Arnold dead. His first concerns are quieting Rachel and concealing her guilt. So he takes Arnold's letter confessing his love for Christian (about which the couple had been quarreling) and burns it. Then he picks up the fireplace poker and tries to wash off the matted hair and blood, leaving his fingerprints on the poker. Advising Rachel to tell

## MAJOR WORKS OF THE MIDDLE PERIOD (1968–1973)

the police that it was an accident, Pearson calls for an ambulance and the police. When the police arrive, naive, gullible, and self-centered Bradley acts very guilty. Bradley is condemned by his behavior; Rachel has only to act the grieving wife and let the police take it from there.

Logically, Bradley should have expected Rachel's behavior. He knew that he had "earned Rachel's undying hate" (p. 247) and that "Rachel was not a forgiver" (p. 247), but he sees a kind of perfection in the way things turned out: "She had taken such a perfect revenge upon the two men in her life" (p. 332). Ironically, Bradley is actually condemned for his failure to love, his failure to see others as they are. He certainly should have seen Rachel's forewarnings. Soon after Rachel had proclaimed her love for Bradley and extracted a pledge of lifelong fidelity (halfheartedly given just to get rid of her), Bradley fell in love with Rachel's daughter, Julian. Bradley then tried to ease himself away from Rachel, but she told him prophetically;

> "You know there's a lot of fire in me. I'm not a wreck like poor old Priscilla. A lot of fire and power yet. Yes."
> "Of course—" [Pearson responded distractedly].
> "You don't understand," [warned Rachel], "I don't mean anything to do with simplicity and love. I don't even mean a will to survive. I mean *fire, fire*. What tortures. What kills." (p. 150)

Bradley recalls these words after his conviction.

Bradley is also morally culpable for his sister's suicide. She had gone to her brother for help, but Pearson did not want to alter his plans and left her in the charge of the unreliable Francis Marloe. Feeling distraught and unloved, Priscilla committed suicide on the night of Pearson's elopement with Julian.

The subtitle of Bradley Pearson's novel, *A Celebration of Love,* indicates that through the painful process of loss of self Bradley has achieved truth. The self-absorbed artist that readers meet at the beginning of the novel could not have produced this work; his suffering dispels his illusions about himself, and he learns to recognize others. Though short-lived, his love affair with Julian has allowed him to open himself to others and to the pain that comes with such involvement.

The postscripts which follow the novel are a clever and convincing extension of the closely structured plot and are consistent with the characterization developed in the novel. Christian, Bradley's ex-wife, concludes that Bradley is mentally ill; her signature reveals that she has now married Bradley's friend from the civil service, Hartbourne. Francis Marloe, the quack psychiatrist, gives a Freudian reading of the story and claims that Bradley was actually in love with Arnold rather than his daughter. His postscript reveals that a subscription list for his forthcoming work, *Bradley Pearson, the Paranoiac from the Paper Shop,* is now open in care of the publisher. Rachel Baffin's postscript belittles Pearson and claims that her daughter once called him ''the family pussycat.'' Rachel denies that she or her daughter ever felt any love for Pearson and says his claims were merely fantasy on his part. She insists that she and her husband had known for a number of years that Pearson had been in love with her. Julian's postscript admits that she loved her father, but her

## MAJOR WORKS OF THE MIDDLE PERIOD (1968–1973)

feelings for Pearson seem muddled: "I think the child I was loved the man Pearson was. But this was a love which words cannot describe" (p. 361). She has, however, become a poet and has adopted the same errant aesthetic views which Pearson had professed: "A poet who is a novelist's child must deplore the parent's verbosity" (p. 359).

Finally, the "Editor's Postscript" discloses Pearson's death and critiques the other postscripts, pointing out each individual's egoistic concerns. P. Loxias, Apollo—the god of art and Eros—directs the reader back to the truth which great art can reveal, if the reader will attend properly. Murdoch, for her part, has presented all of the pieces to the puzzle: she has created fully rounded characters who are convincing and culpable; she has played off the possibilities and probabilities in the postscripts and then shown the postscripts to be the unreliable egoistic extensions of their writers.[23] Ultimately she has presented a very satisfying literary and popular novel which takes up the aesthetics of its author: "Art is not cosy and it is not mocked. Art tells the only truth that ultimately matters. It is the light by which human things can be mended. And after art there is, let me assure you all, nothing" (p. 366).

### Notes

1. Iris Murdoch, *The Nice and the Good* (New York: Viking, 1968), p. 29; subsequent references to this work are noted parenthetically in the text.

2. Homan Potterton's *The National Gallery: London* (London: Thames and Hudson, 1977), p. 72.

3. Diana Phillips, "The Complementarity of Good and Evil in *A Fairly Honourable Defeat*," in *Encounters with Iris Murdoch*, ed. Richard Todd (Amsterdam: Free University Press, 1988), p. 86.

4. Ibid., p. 96.

5. Ibid., p. 96.

6. Ibid., p. 97.

7. Peter Conradi, *Iris Murdoch: The Saint and the Artist* (New York: St. Martin's Press, 1986), p. 162.

8. Iris Murdoch, *A Fairly Honourable Defeat* (New York: Viking, 1970), p. 39; subsequent references to this work are noted parenthetically in the text.

9. Jean-Louis Chevalier, ed., *Recontres avec Iris Murdoch* (Caen: Centre de Recherches de Littérature et Linguistique des Pays de Langue Anglaise, 1978), p. 76.

10. Conradi, p. 88.

11. Ibid., p. 169.

12. Iris Murdoch, *The Sovereignty of Good* (New York: Schocken Books, 1971), p. 66.

13. Peter Conradi remarks that Simone Weil (whose work influenced Iris Murdoch) "believed that extreme affliction is passed on by all but the saintly" (p. 169).

14. Chevalier, p. 78.

15. Ibid.

16. Bradley Pearson has homosexual tendencies. At moments of crisis he often rushes outside his flat and glances upward at the phallic post office tower.

17. Chevalier, p. 78.

18. Conradi, p. 284.

19. "Iris Murdoch Talks with Eric Robson," *Revelations*, Border Television for BBC Channel 4, broadcast September 22, 1984.

20. Simon Price, "Iris Murdoch: An Interview with Simon Price," *Omnibus* 7th Issue (March 1984): 3.

21. Price, p. 4.

22. Iris Murdoch, *The Black Prince* (New York: Viking Press, 1973), p. 29; subsequent references to this work are noted parenthetically in the text.

23. Chevalier, p. 78. In her remarks at Caen, Murdoch states her feelings about the veracity of the novel's postscripts: "We certainly can't, I think, altogether believe Julian in her postscript, and can we even believe all that Mr. Loxias himself says, although I think that Mr. Loxias, in saying that art is very much greater than all these definitions which have been offered of it, is right."

# CHAPTER FIVE

# Later Major Works (1978–1980)

### The Sea, The Sea (1978)

Iris Murdoch illustrates gradations of illusion in her 1978 Booker Prize-winning novel, *The Sea, The Sea*. Here the illusion of the theater, Tibetan powers which degenerate into trickery, and fantastic workings of the imagination produce false perceptions which are connected with power and interfere with the characters' desires to become virtuous. A master technician, Murdoch draws from both the theater and art to develop these themes. A striking and realistic set piece at the Wallace Collection provides the iconography for the novel, primarily associating two of the Collection's paintings, Titian's *Perseus and Andromeda* and Rembrandt's *Titus,* with people and events in the novel. The magic and power evident in Shakespeare's *The Tempest* also figure prominently in the plot.

The narrator of the novel, Charles Arrowby, an actor, playwright, and famed director who is known as a "Shakespeare man,"[1] claims to have written this work to repent of his life of egoism (p. 3). Like the aging Prospero in *The Tempest*, Charles hopes to retire from his life of power and magic, and again like Prospero, he finds it difficult to relinquish his manipulation of others.[2]

Throughout his writings, Charles reveals his jealousy of his cousin, James, a Buddhist and a retired general. When the two men are brought together, the reader learns that both strive for a virtuous life, but by different paths. The main topics of this novel revolve about their use of power; the tricks in their lives, though entirely different, prevent their spiritual amelioriation. Charles had enjoyed considerable power as a theater director; in the course of studying Buddhism in Tibet James had developed paranormal powers; both men must relinquish their powers and come to terms with their pasts in order to avoid repeating previous mistakes.

Structurally, Charles's work consists of three parts: "PREHISTORY," "HISTORY," and "POSTSCRIPT: Life Goes On." "PREHISTORY" introduces the reader to his past life and childhood. Charles's jealousy of his cousin is evident from his belittling remarks about James's disappointing life. Speaking with apparent frankness, Charles has nothing better to say about any past loves or friends, all of whom he had treated badly. His first adult love was the actress Clement Makin, now dead, who loved him when she was at least thirty-nine and he was twenty. He received his start in the theater with her help. Then he fell in love with Lizzie Scherer when she played Ariel to his Prospero (p. 38). Although Lizzie was madly in love with Charles, he found it "surprisingly easy to leave her when the time came" (p. 41). Charles also took Rosina Vamburgh away from her husband, Peregrine Arbelow, and then discarded her.

### LATER MAJOR WORKS (1978–1980)

The six-part "HISTORY" section comprises the bulk of Charles's novel, primarily relating the events of the summer when he retired to Shruff End, by the sea. These events lead to his self-discovery. Most of his former friends and lovers reenter his life at Shruff End; Rosina tries to enact some vengance for the way he has treated her by haunting Shruff End, and Peregrine attempts to murder Charles for stealing his wife. The main concern in "HISTORY" is the illusion which Charles harbors that the love of his youth, Mary Hartley Smith Fitch, still loves him. Although Hartley refused to marry him some forty years earlier, the egoistic Charles cannot believe that she ever stopped loving him. After meeting her in the village of Narrowdean, near Shruff End, Charles kidnaps her with the intention of making her change her mind. Charles hopes to woo Hartley by locating her estranged adopted son, Titus, and relies on James's paranormal powers to find Titus and bring him to Shruff End. Although James locates Titus, his powers of concentration are forced beyond his capacity after he levitates himself in order to save Charles from drowning in a caldron into which he has been pushed by Peregrine. While James is recuperating from this exertion, Titus drowns in the sea.

The lives of the Arrowby cousins provide the contexts for Murdoch's consideration of moral and aesthetic issues. Charles Arrowby is closely associated with and recognizes the illusion and deception of the theater, but he is drawn to it because of his egoism: "The theatre is an attack on mankind carried on by magic: to victimize an audience every night, to make them laugh and cry and suffer and miss their trains. Of course actors regard audiences as enemies, to be deceived, drugged, incarcerated, stupefied'' (p. 33).

Because magic and illusion are fundamental to the theater, Charles believes that only great artists can express truth through this art. Comparing his art form to that of the novel, he believes only the very best theatrical works can express verisimilitude but that a mediocre writer expresses some truth because his art has less fantasy than the theater: "Even a middling novelist can tell quite a lot of truth" (p. 33). Thus the contrast between the great artist, who portrays reality through his art, and the mediocre artist, who tells lies, is most apparent in the theater.[3]

The relationship between the spiritual development of the artist and truth is another of the novel's themes. Here the vanity prevalent in the theater, the demands of the theater upon personal life, and the power available to the artist are not consistent with attributes of the good. According to Charles, most actors are vain: "Vanity receives such a battering in the theatre, one would imagine that it would tend to vanish, but most actors manage to retain theirs: not only as an occupational ailment, but perhaps actually as a necessary instrument of survival" (p. 38). Power is also available for the successful, particularly theater directors; Charles feels that the director who is not a dictator is not doing his job (p. 37), and he is certainly perceived as a tyrant by his friends.

The possibilities for truth which exist in the theater require the efforts of a great genius, like Shakespeare, to illuminate the truth as distinct from the magic and illusion: "Only geniuses like Shakespeare conceal the fact [that they are obsessed men], or rather change it into something spiritual'' (p. 34). Peregrine Arbelow, Charles's friend, calls Shakespeare the only artist capable of depicting life as other than a vulgar trick (p. 166). By contrast, Charles, who found his ''reputation for ruthlessness . . . extremely useful'' (p. 37), produces only mediocre art. Charles even admits that he turned to the theater as a substitute for poetry because he lacked the vision for poetry (p. 33). And Peregrine presents a scathing summary of Charles's professional and spiritual failures: ''You never did anything for mankind, you never did a damn thing for anybody except yourself. . . . ''Your work wasn't any bloody good, it was just a pack of pretentious tricks'' (p. 399).

Charles's father had taken him to the Wallace Collection to see Frans Hals's *Laughing Cavalier* when he was young, and Charles associates the collection with his father (p. 169). As he gazes at the portraits years later, he recognizes several of the women in his life: ''They were there: Lizzie by Terborch, Jeanne by Nicholaes Maes, Rita by Domenichino, Rosina by Rubens, a perfectly delightful study by Greuze of Clement as she was when I first met her. . . . There was even a picture of my mother by Reynolds'' (p. 170). When Charles then enters the ''big central gallery,'' his description of Titian's *Perseus and Andromeda* transforms the painting into events from his own life:

> I had been admiring the graceful naked figure of the girl, whose almost dancing pose as she struggles with her chains makes her seem as airborne as her rescuer, when I seemed to notice suddenly, though I had seen

it many times before, the terrible fanged open mouth
of the sea dragon, upon which Perseus was flying
down head first. The sea dragon did not quite resem-
ble my sea monster, but the mouth was very like, and
the memory of that hallucination, or whatever it was,
was suddenly more disquieting than it had ever been
since the first shock of its appearance. I turned
quickly away and found myself face to face with, directly opposite, Rembrandt's picture of Titus. So Titus
was here too. Titus and the sea monster and the stars
and holding Hartley's hand in the cinema over forty
years ago. (p. 171)

It is of course symptomatic of Charles's egoism that he
connects everything and everyone to himself. Charles envisions himself as Perseus rescuing Andromeda (Hartley,
chained to a monotonous existence with her husband, Ben).
But the sea dragon rising up to meet him, whose mouth resembles the sea monster which Charles thought he had seen at
Shruff End, is actually, Charles later realizes, the serpent of
his own jealousy: "I let loose my own demons, not least the
sea serpent of jealousy" (p. 492). Like the jealousy depicted
in Bronzino's *An Allegory,* which Murdoch had used in an earlier novel, *The Nice and the Good,* this serpent is disfigured
and poisonous.

Rembrandt's painting of his son, *Titus,* becomes the son
which Charles could have had with Hartley had they married.
Hartley's husband jealously though wrongly suspects that Ti-

tus may be Charles's son by Hartley, and Titus returns to Shruff End, in part to discover if Charles may indeed be his lost father. Charles wants to take Titus's affections entirely away from the Fitches by adopting Titus and leaving him his money (p. 383). Even Charles's last temptation to continue the mistakes of his past, Angela Godwin's invitation to give him a son, speaks to the egoism of a sterile and aging man who desperately wants to be remembered in the world.

Although Charles Arrowby's egoism is quite evident to the reader, James Arrowby possesses some traits which would ordinarily place him as a spiritually good figure. A Buddhist and vegetarian, James is aware of the principle of unity. He forms a mandala out of rocks on the sea cliff (p. 471) and protects creatures, including moths and flies (p. 444). He also exhibits mature vision and judgment. When Charles kidnaps his childhood sweetheart, James calmly urges rationality and consideration of Hartley's feelings and eventually persuades Charles to return her to her husband.

However, James does fail through the inappropriate use of powers acquired during years of study in Tibet. His vanity had killed his Sherpa servant, Malarepa, whom he had loved. They went on a mountain journey together during the winter, and James thought that his powers of concentration would be enough to keep both of them warm. James was wrong, and Malarepa died in his arms: "It was my vanity that killed him. . . . The payment for a fault is automatic" (p. 447). Further, he tells Charles that this power has nothing to do with spiritual goodness; it is merely a trick that almost anyone can learn. James's misuse of his spiritual powers is a form of deception similar to the magic and illusion of the theater which Charles misuses.

This novel stresses the interconnectedness of all things, the consequences of actions, and the necessity for acting with humility. James's vanity cost him a friend whom he loved and set him, according to Buddhist teachings, back to the wheel to perfect himself. Speaking to Charles about his beliefs, James explains the Tibetan belief in *bardo:* "the souls of the dead, while waiting to be reborn, wander in a sort of limbo, not unlike the Homeric Hades" (p. 384). It is a place of just and automatic punishment (p. 384). When Charles asks if everyone goes to *bardo,* James replies that "you have a chance at the moment of death" to become free of the wheel of reincarnation: "At the moment of death you are given a total vision of all reality which comes to you in a flash. . . . If you can comprehend and grasp it then you are free," he explains, out of the wheel of "attachments, cravings, desires, what chains us to an unreal world" (p. 385).

James had been setting aside the things of this world, preparing for his spiritual journey, death, when he contacted Charles to effect a reconciliation. But this reunion brought, once again, the use of James's paranormal powers. Finally, James recognizes the dangerous appeal of magic:

> All spirituality tends to degenerate into magic, and the use of magic has an automatic nemesis even when the mind has been purified of grosser habits. White magic is black magic. And a less than perfect meddling in

the spiritual world can breed monsters for other people. Demons used for good can hang around and make
mischief afterwards. The last achievement is the absolute surrender of magic itself, the end of what you call
superstition. Yet how does it happen? Goodness is giving up power and acting upon the world negatively.
(p. 445)

James's reliance on power, even for good, precludes spiritual
growth, and he must relinquish his powers in order to attain
spiritual maturity.

After reflection, Charles's mnemonic writing jogs his
memory about his rescue. Once he believes in James's paranormal powers, Charles has an epiphany of sorts: ''I sat down
again at my table, trying to breathe regularly, and at the idea
that my cousin had used some strange power which he possessed to save my life I was suddenly filled with the most
piercing pure and tender joy, as if the sky had opened and a
stream of white light had descended'' (p. 470). Charles immediately feels a different relationship with James and wants
desperately to talk to him. But before he can, Charles receives
a letter from James's Indian physician, P. R. Tsang, telling
him of James's death. The letter seems to indicate that James
has been released from the wheel and has achieved nirvana:

I had some prophetic thought about him, and when I
came to him I saw what had been. In northern India I
have known such deaths, and I tell it to you so that
you need not be sorry too much. Mr Arrowby died in
happiness achieving all. . . . I looked upon him with

reverence and bowed before him. He has gone quietly
and by the force of his own thought was consciousness
extinguished. Thus it is good to go. Believe me, Sir,
he was an enlightened one. (p. 473)

Following James's death, Charles goes down by the sea
and falls asleep. He awakes at dawn, remembers James's
death, thinks about the possibility of James's having been his
first love, and sees, for the first time, the sea lions: "They
curved and played a while, gulping and gurgling a little, looking up at me all the time. And as I watched their play I could
not doubt that they were beneficent beings come to visit me
and bless me" (p. 476). To this point the sea had been fierce
and alien, and the only creatures Charles had seen were the
monsters in his imagination. Now the gentle creatures of the
sea bless him, an indication of some spiritual growth.

While the "POSTSCRIPT" reveals a milder and less ma-
lignant Charles Arrowby, he may or may not be adjusting to a
less egoistic life, for the ending of the novel is ambiguous.
When a miniature casket, left to Charles by James, falls off of
its brackets and onto the floor, Charles becomes alarmed:
"The lid has come off and whatever was inside it has certainly
got out. Upon the demon-ridden pilgrimage of human life,
what next I wonder?" (p. 502). If Charles has indeed been pu-
rified by his experiences, he will not choose to reenter the
"wheel," but a strong temptation draws him back into the
egoism of this world: Angela Godwin, the sixteen-year-old
stepdaughter of Peregrine Arbelow, has written to Charles,
told him she loves him, and offered to give him a son.

## LATER MAJOR WORKS (1978–1980)

### *Nuns and Soldiers* (1980)

The opening chapter of *Nuns and Soldiers* focuses on the dying Guy Openshaw, a kind and generous half-Jewish (now Anglicized) scholar who had studied classics and philosophy at Oxford but later became a civil servant. His suffering illustrates one of the themes of the novel, the suffering of the just.[4] In many ways all of the characters in the novel suffer, but Iris Murdoch questions the ability of their suffering, even Guy's, to rise above the level of consolation and further moral awareness. She makes this point when Guy tells Anne Cavidge that "suffering is always so interesting. [In Christianity] there is pain, and then, hey presto, there is eternal life. That's what we all want, that our misery shall buy something, that we shall get something in return, something absolutely consoling. But it's a lie."[5]

The nuns and soldiers of the title have meaning for the all of the novel's characters who are in some way alienated from the world or soldiering on with their disappointments and duties, but two characters who specifically fulfill these titles are Anne Cavidge, perhaps Iris Murdoch's most assertive good female character, and Wojciech Szczepanski (the Count), who experiences a vicarious identification with the suffering of the Polish freedom-fighters. Anne, a former nun, is a Cambridge friend of Gertrude Openshaw; when her love for the count is not reciprocated, Anne withdraws from the world again by going to Chicago to live and work with the Poor Clares, an external order of nuns. The Count, obsessed with his Polish heritage, has the merits of a good man—idealism, love, kindness, and humility. He envisions himself as a "very ordinary soldier with a soldier's dullness and . . . extremely small chance of glory" (p. 14). His aspirations include behaving correctly (p. 1) and performing his duties. The Count loves Gertrude, Guy's wife, and wants to serve her.

Gathering around to support Guy and Gertrude are a collection of relatives and friends, often referred to as the Ebury Street set. This name denotes not only the Openshaws' address but also their upper-middle-class education and values, which separate them from characters who are peripheral to the group, Tim Reede and his mistress, Daisy Barrett, failed painters who live in Soho, a bohemian area of London. When Tim turns up at the Openshaws' weekly gatherings of "*les cousins et les tantes*," primarily to carry away little bits of bread and butter, cheeses, and oatmeal cakes for his and Daisy's supper, the Count is the only one to notice Tim or show him any courtesy and respect. The other cousins are capable of ignoring both Tim and his financial difficulties.

Ironically, Gertrude's suffering is soon replaced by the consolation of attention. Although she had wondered during Guy's dying how she could "endure so much misery . . . without dying of it" (p. 44), she becomes a Penelope figure following his death, attracting almost all of the available men as suitors. She welcomes this attention, and even after her marriage to Tim Reede, she draws the Count back as her courtly lover. Gertrude's egoism is also indicated by her reaction to Anne's decision to go to America: "Gertrude did not reveal to Tim how very deeply she had been wounded by Anne's defection. How could she leave me, she thought again and again, how *could* she, when I needed her and loved her so much? Oh why can I not have everything, all that was given to me after Guy went'' (p. 472).

This novel is ablaze with contrasts. The prim and conventional drawing room at Ebury Street, where the characters perform much like the orchestra of china monkeys on the Openshaws' marble mantelshelf, is set against the impoverished, artsy world of Tim and Daisy, shown by their Fitzroy Square, Shepherd's Bush, Notting Hill, and Soho associations. These extremes indicate the characters' social and educational differences and highlight their lack of empathy and understanding for one another.

Yet another counterpoint with the closely detailed London settings is the magnificence of the sun-struck wilds of Provence.[6] Here the French landscape is seen as enchanting, and the plotting follows the tradition in which the staid Englishman is captivated and transformed by the more relaxed atmosphere of France. Significantly, this change also involves moral awareness, for Tim Reede experiences an epiphany in France which results in self-knowledge and new direction in his life; however, the reader should question Tim's ability to sustain this vision because it may be above his spiritual level.[7]

Of the two characters who experience epiphanies in the novel, Tim Reede is initially transformed by the French landscape, perhaps primarily because he is removed from his dreary and muddled London existence. He has a two-day-a-week teaching job at a polytechnic in Wellesden and lives on national assistance. Tim's father had left him a small trust in care of the Openshaw banks, and Guy continued to support

Tim after the trust was depleted. Tim's art is derivative and juvenile, and he appears content to be a mediocre painter (p. 80).

Gertrude sends Tim to France after Guy's death because she feels that she must continue to be responsible for him as Guy had been while he was alive. Tim is to become caretaker for the Oppenshaw summer house and arrange for its sale, which may prove difficult since he has lied about his fluency in French. However, the French landscape transforms him and helps him return to serious art. He climbs the rock formations and begins to sketch them. He even feels a sense of spiritual renewal after dipping his fingers in a basin formed by the rocks.

Following this renewal, Tim searches for a place to swim and finds a canal where he experiences a shocking baptism. Once he slides into the moving stream, he is "seized by a water demon" and "abruptly dragged round" and "jerked down" the canal until he finally grabs hold of a "bushy thorny acadia, whose ferny leaves were sweeping the water" (p. 157). He crawls out of the canal just before it enters a subterranean tunnel and descends "into the earth and vanish[es] totally from the sunny landscape" (p. 158).

When a frightened Tim retreats to the safety of the cottage, he finds Gertrude standing on the terrace. She is so removed from awareness of Tim that, although she claims to have been worried that something may have happened to him, she interrupts him three times while he is trying to tell her that something very nearly did happen to him. Gertrude has arrived to revisit and say good-bye to all of her treasured places before selling the house, but before she leaves the enchanting landscape she will swim in the stone basin, become for Tim the goddess of the crystal pool, and become engaged to him.

Once Tim and Gertrude have experienced the enchantment of the crystal pool, their views of each other are altered: Tim looks "a different man from the pallid weedy rather hangdog young fellow who had come to Gertrude with apologetic hints about needing money. He seemed bigger, stronger" (p. 177). To Tim, Gertrude seems "an Arthurian girl, a heroic girl out of a romantic picture" (p. 180).

The next day Tim worries that they have been enchanted by the landscape: "This couldn't have happened at Ebury Street. . . . It's just something to do with here, with this place, this landscape. We're under a spell. But when we go away it will fade. You'll see I'm just a dull fellow with ass's ears" (pp. 186–88).[8] Indeed, their midsummer enchantment is short-lived, for once Gertrude's London set arrives, she begins to lie about their situation, and Tim appears a less impressive figure. They return to London, where they eventually marry, but their relationship continues to be worn by fears and insecurity, including anonymous letters accusing Tim of fortune hunting.[9] Tim flees from Ebury Street, and Gertrude decides to file for divorce.

Eventually Tim returns to Daisy and then finds the fortitude to separate from her for good. Following this decision, he experiences an epiphany in Hyde Park:

> The white light seemed to be with him again but it was different now. . . . He found that he could see

> through it. He could see the trees, the huge quiet
> planes, with their immense friendly peeling trunks and
> the vast dangling swing of their downward reaching
> branches covered with feathery leaves." (p. 388)

However, "the weird amazing joy he had experienced in Hyde Park ebbed from him in the days, indeed in the hours, that followed" (p. 398), so it appears that Tim cannot sustain his revelation. But he does continue to rebuild his life, selling some of his paintings, getting another teaching job, and beginning again with his art by making a number of leaf collages.

Only under the healing powers of the French landscape can the love between Gertrude and Tim be renewed. When Gertrude returns to France, Tim follows her with the intention of reuniting, but he finds her holding hands with the Count and again takes flight. While revisiting their sacred sites, Tim sees an English collie in the canal; as he instinctively reaches out to rescue the animal, he slips into the stream. The two are carried on to the stone tunnel mouth, where Tim expects to be drowned in the tunnel, but both are deposited safely onto the valley beyond.

Following this baptism in the subterranean section of the canal, Tim experiences a clarity of vision often associated with near-death experiences in Murdoch's novels: "Tim blessed the dog, he blessed the open sky and the sun, he even blessed the canal" (p. 424). He then decides to return to Gertrude rather than to seek aid in the village, and they are reconciled. Later, when reflecting on what happened in France, Tim recognizes that "something in his life had begun there, something which tied deeply and mysteriously together Gertrude and his art'' (p. 476).

Anne Cavidge also experiences an epiphany in *Nuns and Soldiers*, but her illumination suggests a more difficult path. Anne, who had been a member of an enclosed religious order for fifteen years, came to stay with Gertrude when she left the convent. Her stay coincided with Guy's final illness. A very capable woman, Anne had received a first-class degree in history from Cambridge (p. 55), but at Ebury Street she feels invisible, unnoticed by others (p. 141). Such a description is often equated with goodness in Murdoch's novels, and Anne does exhibit good behavior. She sets herself the task of helping Gertrude run the household and is able to converse with Guy for hours.

Perhaps the most controversial set piece in any Murdoch novel involves a beatific vision, a visitation from Jesus Christ, which Anne experiences. Anne's vision began as a dream in which she encountered two angels. She woke up and remembered the dream. ''Then again she became aware, she *knew,* that there was somebody in the next room, somebody standing in her kitchen in the bright light of the early summer morning. And she knew that the person was Jesus'' (p. 289). When Anne asked the visitor what she must do to be saved, he replied: ''You must do it all yourself. . . . As for salvation, anything you can think about it is as imaginary as my wounds. I am not a magician, I never was. You know what to do. Do right, refrain from wrong'' (pp. 291–92).

But Anne does not understand fully, for she wants the concessions which ordinary humans expect from the savior;

she wants to be made innocent. He instructed her to wash at the sink. Although Anne followed his directions, she replied, "It's—no good—it—won't work—" and reached out her dripping hands toward him (p. 293). After brushing the sleeve of his shirt, she felt "a searing pain in her hand and her eyes closed and she fell to her knees and then flat to the ground in a sudden faint" (p. 294). When she woke up, her hands were still damp and she had a raw burn on one of the fingers of her right hand, apparently tangible evidence that her vision had been real.

In *Iris Murdoch: The Saint and the Artist,* Peter Conradi correctly concedes that "Murdoch's interest in the supernatural is a problem for some readers" (p. 142). Both of the novels considered in this chapter, *Nuns and Soldiers* and *The Sea, The Sea,* have paranormal incidents, and the incident in *The Sea, The Sea* is clearly connected with Eastern mysticism. Conradi points out that Murdoch has indicated she believes paranormal things probably do happen, but he cautions "this should not obscure for us that what is supernatural for Murdoch is principally the imagination itself, and love in particular."[10]

Anne's illumination concerns her becoming good and doing so by letting go of her consolations: "She had left the convent to come out into loneliness and a sort of renewed innocence and a sort of peace" (p. 303). But once she was in the world, she found that she could not merely perform good works; she also became entangled in muddles of her own, like her love for the Count and the manipulation of others to bring

him closer to her. Now she must relinquish the comforts of human love and faith in order to renew her spiritual journey.

Anne's reliance on faith may be the last consolation that
she must overcome, for only after she is stripped of any consolation can she act alone, without ulterior motives. Indeed, at
the end of the novel she finds herself able to relinquish the
Count and plans to return to a life of service for others with the
Poor Clares. Conversely, Tim's epiphany involves love at a
significantly lower level, for his love will always include an
amount of lifesaving egoism. Tim emerges from the rushing
canal wanting to be comforted by Gertrude. Here, as in all
of Murdoch's novels, awareness distinguishes the levels of
good in her characters. Anne Cavidge has had a terrible vision
of the solitary nature of her quest; she also appears capable
of relinquishing her ego and its attending consolations,
actions which Murdoch deems necessary for association with
the good.

## *Notes*

1. Iris Murdoch, *The Sea, The Sea* (New York: Viking Press, 1978), p.
39; subsequent references to this work are noted parenthetically in the text.
2. For fuller discussions of *The Tempest* motif in *The Sea, The Sea,* see
any of the following works: Elizabeth Dipple, *Iris Murdoch: Work for the
Spirit* (Chicago: University of Chicago Press, 1982); Peter J. Conradi, *Iris
Murdoch: The Saint and the Artist* (New York: St. Martin's Press, 1986);
Lindsey Tucker, "Released from Bonds: Iris Murdoch's Two Prosperos in *The*

## UNDERSTANDING IRIS MURDOCH

Sea, The Sea,'' Contemporary Literature 27, no. 3 (1986): 378–95; Rosemary Dinnage, "The Corruption of Love," New York Review of Books 26 (February 8, 1979): 20–21.

3. The danger of art as fantasy is one of the reasons given for the low esteem of the artist in Plato's Republic; this topic is the central theme of Murdoch's The Fire and the Sun: Why Plato Banished the Artists (Oxford: Oxford University Press, 1977).

4. See also The Unicorn, in which suffering as consolation is a major theme.

5. Iris Murdoch, Nuns and Soldiers (New York: Viking Press, 1980), p. 66; subsequent references to this work are noted parenthetically in the text.

6. Contrast the mythic French landscape shown in Nuns and Soldiers with the frenzied carnivalesque Paris of Iris Murdoch's youth, brilliantly shown in Under the Net. Nuns and Soldiers is dedicated to Stephen and Natasha Spender, whose Provence farmhouse provides the setting for the French chapters. The house, called Les Grandes Saules in the novel, is a near replica of the Spenders' converted red-tiled stone farmhouse where John Bayley and Iris Murdoch often visit. Photographs of the house and landscape appear in "An Afternoon with the Woodpeckers," W (October 18–25, 1985): 54–55. Mountains and rock formations appear in the distance; an olive grove and a canal actually exist.

7. Murdoch comments on the relationship between a character's inability to sustain awareness and that character's level of spirituality in a discussion of The Unicorn at a symposium at Caen University. See "Discussion sur The Unicorn," Gaéliana no. 5 (Caen: Centre de Recherches de Littérature, Linguistique et Civilisation des Pays de Langue Anglaise de l'Université de Caen, 1983), pp. 195–210. The discussion is in English.

8. Murdoch makes fairly direct references to William Shakespeare's A Midsummer Night's Dream in this section of the novel. The time is midsummer; the setting is enchanting; Tim falls in love with Gertrude following a dream; the man with ass's ears is Shakespeare's character Bottom.

9. Peter Conradi points out the close association of Nuns and Soldiers and Henry James's The Wings of the Dove in Iris Murdoch: The Saint and the Artist (New York: St. Martin's Press, 1986), p. 265.

10. Conradi, p. 142.

# CHAPTER SIX

# Latest Works (1983–1989)

### *The Philosopher's Pupil* (1983)

With *The Philosopher's Pupil* Iris Murdoch begins a series of lengthy commentaries upon art and life which present a mature reevaluation of the complexities of her vision. The reader finds in these current works a sense of adjustment and summary. In *The Philosopher's Pupil* the philosopher John Robert Rozanov returns home to Ennistone to refine his understanding of philosophy and complete his great work on moral philosophy.[1] *The Good Apprentice* reveals the extraordinary and difficult path to virtue in the modern world. *The Book and the Brotherhood* concerns a group of left-wing, middle-aged Oxford friends, former Marxists, who reconsider their financial support of a Marxist writer whose views they no longer believe.[2] And *The Message to the Planet*, as the didactic title implies, reiterates the necessity for goodness in a contingent and accidental world. All of these novels demonstrate the interconnected nature of all life and the futility of attaching ourselves to substitute gods.

*The Philosopher's Pupil* continues the moral concerns of
Murdoch's earlier novels—freedom, forgiveness, and goodness—and its length is conducive to complicated machinations
and extensive character development. The Shakespearean
match in the younger generation between Hattie Meynell,
Rozanov's grandchild, and Tom McCaffrey, the son of Alan
McCaffrey and "Feckless" Fiona, gives the novel an almost
enchanting air. Hattie's residence in the Slipper House and the
ritual played out by the young cast of the masque *The Triumph
of Aphrodite* support this reading. However, the more serious
matters about which this discussion will center are Murdoch's
interests in moral improvement, artistic duty, and religion.
The dilemma which faces the artist who would also be good
is shown through John Robert Rozanov and his relations with
the title character, George McCaffrey, and with his grandchild, Hattie; Father Jacoby's eccentric religious beliefs are revealed in a dialectic with Rozanov; and a figure of the good,
William Eastcote, expresses Quaker humility and the necessity
for love.

The novel makes extensive use of water imagery through
its setting, the fictional Ennistone, which is situated on the
River Enn and famous for its Roman springs. All of the Ennistone inhabitants are water-lovers who meet daily at the spa
buildings. The waters are restorative and healing for most.
Alex McCaffrey, for example, cannot speak to or touch her
grandson, Adam, on land, but is able to play with him and
communicate with him in the water.[3] However, the steam and
heat present an inferno of sorts for Tom McCaffrey when he is
locked in the Baptistry (boiler rooms) of the hot springs. There

is something magical about the town, with its ancient Roman associations, megaliths, and the masque which is performed at the springs. Gypsies and flying saucer sightings extend Ennistone's connection with the supernatural.

The novel opens with George McCaffrey, the title character, attempting to murder his wife, Stella, by pushing their car into a canal following an accident. Mentally deranged and subject to fantasies, McCaffrey dreams about killing Stella in this manner, but the dream is actually reality. A failed artist, McCaffrey has lived a life of frustrated ambition (p. 75). He studied philosophy, history, and archaeology and took a first-class degree but failed to obtain the teaching post he wanted. He wrote plays which were not performed and poems that were not published. His one published volume, *A Short History of the Ennistone Museum,* is described as "well written but necessarily of limited importance" (p. 75).

A more malevolent version of Austin Gibson Grey (*An Accidental Man*), George McCaffrey suffers from a form of split personality and claims that he sees his double, who is responsible for his violence (p. 511). He displays his violent nature by attempting to murder Stella; attacking passersby; destroying the Roman glass collection of the Ennistone museum; and smashing one of Stella's collection of Japanese netsuke, which were "tokens of her father's love" (p. 138). He had intended to smash the entire collection, but she had taken them away with her following the "accident."

The search for the father, which is a consistent theme in the later novels, is expressed here and perhaps in some ways explains McCaffrey's behavior. His father had deserted his wife and family for another woman, and McCaffrey is now obsessed with his former teacher, the philosopher John Robert Rozanov, as a father-substitute. He feels that his life can become whole again if he can make Rozanov notice him. But when Rozanov coldly and utterly rejects any connection between them, McCaffrey takes Rozanov's letter as a sign "that his relation with John Robert had reached a final organism" (p. 460). Believing that "love and death [are] interchangeable," McCaffrey attempts to drown Rozanov in the baths (p. 552), forcing a connection similar to that between the German philosopher Moritz Schlick and his pupil.[4]

Because Rozanov had already committed suicide when McCaffrey dumped him in the scalding bath, McCaffrey's attempt to force this connection with Rozanov apparently fails. However, most of the novel's other characters view Rozanov's death as the event which changes McCaffrey's life (p. 563), though the quality of the change is enigmatic and not fully established. On the night of Rozanov's death, McCaffrey sees a flying saucer (already spotted by William Eastcote) flying low over the village common: "As it came it emitted a ray which entered into his eyes and a black utter darkness came upon him and he fell to his knees and lay stretched out senseless in the long grass" (p. 557). For Murdoch, flying saucers signify the interconnectedness of all life, and usually it is only her clearly good characters who make such sightings (Eastcote in this novel and the twins in *The Nice and the Good*). Once he has recovered his sight, McCaffrey becomes quiet and docile. His sister-in-law, Gabriel, describes him as "spiritless, characterless and good," but she also considers him "broken" (p.

573). When McCaffrey's wife returns to him, she finds him "looking over his old plays which had evidently not been destroyed after all" (p. 565), and eventually he begins to write poetry again (p. 574). While McCaffrey's reflections on his mental state reveal "a considerable capacity for self-knowledge" (p. 574), the reader would need additional information about his future actions to establish any pervasive spiritual change.

Iris Murdoch's interest in the dilemma which artists face when they must consider their duty to their art and their duty to others is developed through Rozanov. Rozanov, who returns home to Ennistone to complete his great work on moral philosophy, wishes throughout the novel that he had more time to refine his understanding of philosophy and refuses to allow others to intrude upon his time. Following the early death of his wife, Linda, Rozanov ignored his daughter and concentrated on his publications. When his daughter also died, leaving her daughter, Hattie, Rozanov absolved himself of personal responsibility for his grandchild by hiring a governess and later by sending Hattie away to private schools and trying to arrange for her marriage. While Rozanov provides for Hattie's material needs, he is unavailable for her emotional needs. He devotes himself entirely to philosophy and writing, and his grandchild wonders how often Rozanov remembers that she and her governess even exist (p. 438).

George McCaffrey's desperate desire to further his connection with Rozanov is yet another demand upon the philosopher's time. "George had been attempting for years to attract John Robert's attention, to provide a 'happening' which would establish a 'bond' between them'' (p. 427). He repeatedly asks Rozanov to give him attention: "Can't you even *look* at me, can't you concentrate on me for a moment?" (p. 145). But Rozanov makes it patently clear that he has no time for George: "You keep imagining I think about you, I don't" (p. 222); "As far as I'm concerned you don't exist" (p. 224). Clearly Rozanov is very defensive against all intrusions upon his art.

While Murdoch recognizes the paradox involved in connecting great art with virtue, she has stated that each case must be considered individually to determine if the egoism involved in artistic duty interferes with the truth which art can reveal. *The Fire and the Sun* also makes the point that virtue can lie entirely in the work of art.[5] In Rozanov's case, the protection against intrusion on his time for his art is carried to the extreme. He ignores his responsibilities to his daughter and grandchild and fails to attend to the existence of others or even to converse with anyone unless he initiates the conversation. Even his late interest in Hattie is solipsistic and, as he reveals to Hattie, carnal in nature (pp. 470–71). Accordingly, his work and achievement are less than he expects. After his suicide, Rozanov's fears concerning the failure inherent in his work are confirmed: "Hattie had perhaps not been mistaken in thinking that he was in a state of destructive despair about what he felt to be the failure of his philosophical works" (p. 560).

Murdoch does not have conventional Christian beliefs and appears most comfortable with a mixture of Christian and Buddhist tenets.[6] As a result, she presents her readers with some quite eccentric religious figures who are unorthodox and universal in their doctrine. In *The Philosopher's Pupil*, Father

### LATEST WORKS (1983–1989)

Jacoby is such a figure. A former Jew, Father Jacoby is now a very high Anglican priest who uses incense and often says mass in Latin. Although he no longer believes in God, he continues to meditate, using a mixture of Christian and Buddhist beliefs. A dialectic, an intellectual exercise whose aim is discovery of truth, which takes place between Father Jacoby and Rozanov establishes some of the priest's metaphysical beliefs.[7] Father Jacoby does not believe in a personal God, but he believes in a spiritual reality (p. 185). We live in an "interregnum," a time when spirits exist but one no longer believes in God, he tells Rozanov (p. 187). The major challenge of our age is "just to hang on . . . until religion can change itself into something we can believe in" (p. 187).

Following Rozanov's death, Father Jacoby asks for laicization and goes to Greece, where he has a religious experience which leads him to the conclusion that "the essential and only question of our age [is] the absolute denial of God" (p. 570). He had planned to spend the rest of his life "as a servant in some remote monastery on Mount Athos" (p. 567), but he found it impossible to get along with the holy men at the monastery and moved to a stone chapel in a cave in the Greek countryside.

Although William Eastcote presents views on good and becoming good which are in many ways similar to those of Father Jacoby, the two men have diametrical methods. The cassock, incense, rituals, and tortured metaphysical doubts surrounding Father Jacoby stand in stark contrast to Eastcote's simple declaration of faith (p. 199) and the Quaker Meeting House with its "douce blank Quaker rites" which he attends. Instead of the dialectic of doubt professed by Father Jacoby and Rozanov, Eastcote speaks confidently about humility and love: "Let us love the close things, the close clear good things, and hope that in their light other goods may be added. . . . Let us then seek aid in pure things, turning our minds to good people, to our best work, to beautiful and noble art. . . ." (pp. 204–05).

A revered and gentle person who performs good works, counsels wisely, speaks ill of no one, Eastcote inspires good behavior in his fellow characters by this speech (p. 205). Father Jacoby, on the other hand, is unable to meet the spiritual needs of his parish despite his good intentions. While some critics feel that Iris Murdoch is being unnecessarily harsh on religious figures in her later novels, particularly through the characters of Father Jacoby in this novel and Father McAlister in *The Book and the Brotherhood,* she presents their eccentric beliefs as resulting from the metaphysical dilemma brought about by a loss of faith. And in William Eastcote she offers a positive model for quiet conviction.

One of Murdoch's few good characters, Eastcote possesses Quaker humility and is a proponent of the Friends' belief that "truthful vision spontaneously . . . prompts virtuous desire" (p. 54). At various times Murdoch refers to Eastcote as "a most respected citizen and pillar of the Friends' Meeting House," "a very devout person and pillar of the Meeting," and a "good man" (pp. 27, 53, 454). Dr. Roach calls him "a saint if ever there was one" (p. 431) and, when announcing Eastcote's death, exclaims, "But what a wonderful life, what a wonderful man, not just a comforter but a living evidence of a religious truth" (p. 432).

Indeed, Eastcote's passing is mourned by the many whose lives he has touched. *The Gazette,* reporting on his funeral, cites "the universal respect and affection in which he was held evidenced . . . [by the crowd which] stood in complete and impressive silence . . . to reminisce about the good deeds of the deceased" (pp. 486–87). And "the McCaffrey contingent . . . were all in different ways deeply grieved at the death of one whom they had always regarded as an example of goodness and a place of healing" (p. 487). Even unnatural signs accompany Eastcote's death. The latest saucer sighting appears on the night of his death (p. 488), and Lud's Rill becomes a powerful geyser after his funeral (p. 488).

The collective observations concerning Eastcote's spirituality make him appear larger than humanly possible. But surrounded by a novel of egocentrics, he appears a genuinely loveable person who possesses both knowledge and respect for others. His message rings of simple truths and universal harmony. The first person to view the flying saucer, Eastcote recognizes in it the interconnected nature of all things: "He felt it was something good—a wholly good visitation" (p. 194). And his life is an example of what Murdoch means about becoming virtuous by looking upon good things.

### *The Good Apprentice* (1985)

Forgiveness and healing through the acceptance of responsibility are the subjects of *The Good Apprentice,* a painful work about the consequences of failure to attend to others. The referent of the book's title is ambiguous, with critics assigning the title role to both Edward Baltram and Stuart Cuno.[8] Stuart, much like Murdoch envisions Plato to have been, is an absolutist who exasperates his friends with his moral talk and his refusal to be practical. He has given up a coveted teaching post at a London college in order to lead a moral life, but he does not believe in God.[9] Establishing morality in a world without God is a primary theme in Murdoch's works, and withdrawing from the world is one way toward goodness.

But there are multiple ways to truth, and the novel's action centers on Stuart's stepbrother, Edward Baltram, who is suffering from guilt and depression over an incident which has taken his will to live. Baltram is responsible for the death of his close friend Mark Wilsden. He had slipped a drug into Mark's sandwich and had then watched as Mark experienced what Edward felt would be a "happy journey." Then, after Mark fell asleep, Edward agreed to meet Sarah Plowmain and locked his sleeping friend in their flat. When he returned, he found the window in their flat open and Mark's crushed body on the pavement below. For Edward, Mark's death signifies the wretched ending of all past innocence and promises a future forever maimed by the manner of its loss.

Edward is the son of the painter Jesse Baltram and his favorite model, Chloe Warriston. Jesse had abandoned Chloe before Edward was born, and she then married Harry Cuno, who reared Edward as his own son when Chloe died soon after Edward's birth. Such connections, in addition to complicating the plot, illustrate Murdoch's interest in the interconnected nature of life. A brief summary of the characters' relationships to one another may help clarify the novel. Jesse Baltram, described as a Don Juan (p. 5), fathered Edward with Chloe; he also fathered Betinna and perhaps Ilona with his wife May. Baltram, a bisexual, also had another lover, the painter Max Point. May, who suffered for years because of her husband's promiscuity, is said to have gotten even with him by taking Point as her lover. Max Point may be the father of Ilona, a detail which becomes important when Ilona falls in love with Edward. When Edward's mother, Chloe, married Harry Cuno, Cuno already had a son, Stuart, by his first wife, Teresa, who died from leukemia soon after Stuart's birth (p. 14). The two apprentices to goodness, then, are motherless stepbrothers.

Another family central to the plot is also related to the Baltrams and the Cunos. Midge Warriston McCaskerville, Chloe's elder sister, is married to Thomas McCaskerville, the psychiatrist who tries to help Edward overcome his severe depression following his friend's death. Midge has been having an affair with her former brother-in-law, Harry Cuno (who is also her husband's best friend), but she cannot make up her mind to leave her husband for him. She is also fascinated by Jesse Baltram, possibly because of her sister Chloe's relationship with him. The McCaskervilles have a thirteen-year-old son, Meredith, whom they often ignore. Meredith has a special relationship with Stuart Cuno, who, in his own quiet way, tries to give the boy a sense of self-worth.

Although Stuart and Edward are not close, Edward wants to meet Stuart again and find out what he is like. When Edward explains his relationship with Stuart to Sarah Plowmain, she replies, "So Stuart and you aren't really brothers" (p. 5).

## UNDERSTANDING IRIS MURDOCH

But Edward insists that they have a family connection: "Not blood relations—but, well, we are brothers" (p. 5). This insistence that such a nonblood relation is still family indicates a redemptive process for Edward, who identifies with the title of Part One of the novel: "The Prodigal Son" (p. 1).

Here Murdoch's use of biblical allusion does not indicate a straightforward reading of the text. The novel begins, "I will arise and go to my father, and will say unto him, Father I have sinned against heaven and before thee, and am no more worthy to be called thy son" (p. 1). After attending a seance in which he received a message telling him to seek spiritual healing from his natural father, Edward began searching for the father who had deserted him.

But Edward's understanding of his position is ironic. His healing can begin only when he reconciles with his father and begins to take care of him. In doing so he focuses on the needs of others, and his attention is drawn away from his own anguish and grief. He is then able to seek forgiveness from Mark's sister, Brenda, and she acts as a redemptive force in his life. But Edward's true salvation comes from learning to love and to accept responsibility in his life when he seems to have lost everything. After his father's death and Brenda's engagement to Giles Brightwalton, Edward feels dead himself (p. 511). Then he perceives his place in the world and his connection to others:

> He uncrumpled the letter from Sarah, understanding it for the first time. The letter smelt of incense and brought back that little dark room where Sarah had

## LATEST WORKS (1983–1989)

seduced him while Mark Wilsden's life was being
taken away. . . . Perhaps Mark bound him to Sarah
as he bound him to Brownie [Brenda Wilsden]. He
thought, I have a responsibility to her, I'm responsible
for her, she's unhappy, I must go to her; and he felt
a stirring of curiosity, so often a motive to benevo-
lence. (p. 516)

In a similar manner, a postcard from Ilona arrives from Paris
and reminds him of his responsibility to her: "She would soon
be back, he would meet the new strange Ilona, and they would
talk and talk about their adventures, and in the future he would
*look after her;* after all he was her elder brother" (p. 518). Out
of the depths of despair and isolation, Edward Baltram is
saved by his ability to love and care for others.

Stuart Cuno's approach to goodness, while just as difficult, is not as painful; nor perhaps, in keeping with Murdoch's
other presentations of good characters, is it as interesting for
the reader. Thomas McCaskerville tells Stuart, "You want to
be like the Prodigal Son's elder brother, the chap who never
went away!" (p. 147). And Stuart replies, "Exactly—except
that he was cross when his brother was forgiven" (p. 147).
Even had the biblical elder brother not resented his brother's
return to the family, he would still be the less interesting figure
to the reader because he only stayed home and performed
his duties.

Initially Stuart's action as the dutiful elder brother, his interference in the moral lives of his family members, is not ap-
preciated by them. Stuart feels his connection with Edward is

absolute and that he has a duty to help him recover from Mark Wilsden's death (p. 51); however, he is at first unable to relieve Edward's suffering. So Stuart visits Mrs. Wilsden and tries to persuade her to stop writing hateful letters to Edward. This visit appears to have done no good, for she responds: "He [Edward] has done me terrible damage, destroyed my life and my joy, and done so deliberately. I am surprised that you dare to come here and torture me by mentioning his name. You are more than impertinent, you are sadistic and cruel. . . . Now please leave my house" (p. 388). Stuart's efforts on Meredith's behalf to save Meredith's parents' marriage also result in Stuart's rejection by his father (p. 442), who feels he has lost his mistress, Midge.

Following the rejection by his father, Stuart goes into a church but finds himself unable to pray or even untangle his ideas about moral duty (p. 442). He then begins walking and goes into an Underground station at Oxford Circus, where he experiences a sense of isolation and futility in his life. At that point he happens to look down into the pit at the train tracks and see a mouse: "The mouse ran a little way along beside the wall of the pit, then stopped and sat up. It was eating something. Then it came back again, casting about. It was in no hurry. It was not trapped. *It lived there*" (p. 447). This last thought came as a revelation to Stuart, and he experienced a "peaceful joy" at recognizing his place in the world (p. 447).

It also appears that Stuart's good intentions were not entirely without results. When Mrs. Wilsden is finally able to imagine Edward's state of mind, she pities him (p. 504) and writes him a letter of forgiveness, telling him in a postscript,

## LATEST WORKS (1983–1989)

"Your brother's visit did some good. Tell him" (p. 504). The McCaskervilles reconcile, and Harry Cuno is able to forgive his son for showing Midge her duty. But Stuart's future plans are for proselytizing the younger generation. He tells Edward that he plans to take a teacher training course and teach young children so that he can start them out right: "You can teach language and literature and how to use words so as to *think*. And you can teach moral values, you can teach meditation, what used to be called prayer, and give them an idea of what goodness is, and how to love it" (p. 520).

### *The Book and the Brotherhood* (1987)

Possibly the strongest and most successful of Murdoch's latest novel's, *The Book and the Brotherhood* is a well-paced, dynamic work which brings together parts of her Oxford past. The novel opens with an Oxford Commem Ball, where a circle of Oxford friends, now middle-aged, evaluate their lives and reconsider the politics of their youth and their financial support of one member of their group, David Crimond, who is writing a Marxist book. Speaking of *The Book and the Brotherhood,* Murdoch has said, "It concerned the way in which differences of opinion define people; the notion of a book which at one time everyone felt was going to express their views and later on realized it wasn't."[10] In a touching set piece, this work also illustrates the "remembrance of things past." During the Commem Ball, Gerard Hernshaw returns to visit his former classics professor, Levquist, who asks him to read aloud from the *Iliad*. Gerard chooses the passage in which the immortal horses weep at the death of Patroclus, and both Levquist and Gerard remember the genius and promise of Sinclair Curtland, Gerard's former Oxford friend and lover who had died at a young age in a glider accident.

David Crimond, who has "retained the extreme left-wing idealism which . . . [their set] had once shared,"[11] has spent his life writing a great work about Marxism. In order to free his time for this work, some of the Oxford friends have formed a *Gesellschaft* (financial support group) for him. But Crimond, a demon figure, has alienated the group by his absolutism and by his behavior, and they increasingly find themselves ideologically opposed to his message. In addition to Gerard, the people supporting Crimond include Sinclair's sister, Rose, Jenkin Riderhood, and Gulliver Ashe. Rose, who is in love with Gerard, has been waiting for thirty years for him to notice her: "Her life always seemed so provisional, a waiting life, not settled like other people" (p. 227). Jenkin, considered the least successful of the original set, is a senior history master in a London school (p. 12). But his attributes suggest that he is a good man, and his former Oxford tutor, Levquist says: "Riderhood doesn't need to get anywhere. He walks the path, he exists where he is" (p. 578). New to the group, Gulliver Ashe is a failed artist who is unemployed and "possibly unemployable" (p. 138). Gulliver leads a lonely and solitary life but is saved, perhaps, through a universal experience at King's Cross Station (p. 597).

Other Oxford friends include Duncan Cambus and his wife, Jean Kowitz, who had once left her husband for Cri-

## LATEST WORKS (1983–1989)

mond. Duncan, formerly a distinguished career diplomat, had his vision impaired by a fall down a tower stairs during a fight with Crimond over Crimond's affair with Jean. Jean has a self-destructive attraction to Crimond, and Gerard considers Jean "a woman suitable to be . . . [Crimond's] mate" (p. 344). Crimond manages to take Jean away from Duncan for a second time at the Commem Ball, and their suicide pact (driving their cars into each other at high speed on the Roman road near Rose's country estate), is an absorbing dramatic piece which evidences Iris Murdoch's skill at mechanical descriptions.

The good figure in this novel, Jenkin Riderhood, hates lies and muddles and is "intensely aware of the reality" of others (p. 135). Jenkin no longer believes in a traditional God, but he illustrates the necessity for good works. He identifies with lonely people (p. 135) and is always there for anyone who needs him. Christianity, loss of faith, and attempts to change religion into something intellectual had preceeded his simple acceptance of the necessity for moral behavior. Like most of Murdoch's good figures who no longer believe in God, Jenkin would like to keep religion for its moral structure: "I think it matters what happens to religion, I don't mean supernatural beliefs of course. We must keep some sort of idea of deep moral structure" (p. 249).

Jenkin thinks about going away to Africa or South America, where he can be of more service to others, and Gerard worries that something will happen to him (p. 279). This premonition comes true when Crimond invites Duncan Cambus to a duel over Jean, and Jenkin, who has rushed over to Crimond's to stop them, receives the bullet which Crimond had intended for himself. In yet another suicide attempt, Crimond had filled his own gun with blanks and given Duncan a loaded gun. So Jenkin becomes the sacrificial victim who eventually reunites Duncan and Jean.

The woman's social situation is demonstrated in *The Book and the Brotherhood* through Tamar Hernshaw, a young student forced to leave Oxford to go to work to support her mother, Violet, who is incapable of holding a job. In an effort to comfort Duncan, crazed with depression after Jean leaves him a second time for Crimond, Tamar goes to bed with him. Although Duncan has assured her that he was sterile, Tamar becomes pregnant. Herself an illegitimate and unwanted child, she decides to have an abortion. But following the abortion, she becomes a maimed creature, crippled by guilt: "Nobody *can* love me. It's impossible. I'm a person *outside* love, and I have *always been*" (p. 370).

The only people who seem to care for Tamar or try to help her out of her despair are Jenkin Riderhood and Angus McAlister, another of Murdoch's curious, unbelieving priests. McAlister, the local vicar near Rose's country home, Boyars, is described by Rose as "a bit dotty": "He uses the old prayer book and wants to be 'Father', he even hears confessions!— but he's very evangelical too" (p. 258). This strange combination comes from his having adopted both of his parents' beliefs: "His father had been a High Anglican clergyman, his mother a devout Methodist. . . . His God was that of his father, but his Christ was that of his mother. He spoke the dignified and beautiful language of a reticent spirituality, but he breathed the fire of instant salvation (p. 494). Father McAlis-

## LATEST WORKS (1983–1989)

ter is yet another priest who combines the dogma of various religious groups in a time of shifting faith.

When Tamar, who is certainly seared in spirit, visits the village church, she hears Father McAlister's homily about forgiveness: "The Lord is with the poor, the broken ones whose contrite tears acknowledge that they are nothing" (p. 284). After the service the priest follows the Boyars group and asks to speak to Tamar because he recognizes that she is in grief: "You look as if you are in mourning. Have you lost a loved one?" (p. 287). Tamar thinks his efforts are ridiculous, but as she rises to leave he takes a firm hold of her wrist: "I want you to know that you have a Saviour to whom *nothing is impossible*. You need love. Perhaps you need forgiveness. You need healing. Turn to the boundless perfect love which heals and pardons. Kneel, Tamar" (p. 288). She then tells him her problems (pp. 288–89).

Father McAlister counsels Tamar several times, and he hopes that she will be baptized and confirmed. But his talk about "accepting Christ as her Saviour" seems "to her like the gabble of a witch doctor" (p. 492). However, when Jenkin Riderhood is accidentally shot and killed by David Crimond, Tamar feels that her association with Jenkin has killed him, "and henceforth and forever anyone who came near her would be cursed and destroyed" (p. 493). Surprisingly, she then turns to Father McAlister and accepts his belief that religion can help her, but she appears primarily attracted to the magic in religion. After Father McAlister performs "a kind of burial or blessing of the dead child, a formal affirmation of love and farewell, containing an act of contrition" (p. 498), Tamar is less frightened of the child's spirit, and she finds the determination to make a life for herself.

Unfortunately, Tamar's assertion of self involves a willingness to use power. And when Tamar informs her mother that she is moving out and that she will no longer support her, Father McAlister becomes concerned with Tamar's change:

> Her misery had been genuine, her obsession terrible.
> But in her desperation had she not *used* him as he
> came to hand, carrying out his instruction, as a savage
> might those of a medicine man, or as a sick patient
> obeys a doctor? . . . It was her freedom she had
> wanted, perhaps all along. . . . Have I liberated her
> not into Christ, but into selfish uncaring power?
> (p. 515–16)

The rediscovery of the ego, for Murdoch, is not a form of love or goodness, and Tamar has used the magic in religion for the wrong salvation.

An object of hatred, love, and scorn by his former friends who are all, in some way, obsessed with him, David Crimond appears a larger than life, violent demon figure throughout most of the novel. Jenkin reminds Gerard, "Remember how we all once saw him as the modern man, the hero of our time, we admired him for being so dedicated" (p. 129). But Gerard calls Crimond a "charlatan" and says he doesn't really care about the oppressed (p. 129).

Crimond's book is often the topic of conversation and supposition, but the reader has little indication of its actual merit. The members of the *Gesellschaft* agree to ask Crimond

for a meeting about the book, and Gerard puts their reserva-
tion to him: "You've been writing this book for years and
years and we don't know what's in it! In a sense we've been
responsible for it, we'll be regarded as having sort of commissioned it, and as agreeing with it!" (p. 293). Both Gerard and
Jenkin imagine that the book will be brilliant but based on a
mistake (pp. 299, 343). The clearest description which Gerard
is able to give of the book is to say that it explains all of
philosophy:

> . . . that's what he's done, the preSocratics, Plato,
> Aristotle, Plotinus, right up to the present, and East-
> ern philosophy too—and that means morality, religion,
> art, it all comes in, there's a splendid chapter on Au-
> gustine, and he writes so well, it's funny and witty, all
> sorts of people will read it—. (p. 560)

Crimond's great work is similar to a number of life works
undertaken by intellectuals in Murdoch's novels.[12] Ultimately,
however, the other authors find themselves incapable of ex-
pressing their visions. Crimond, whose genius no one doubts,
has alienated himself from the mainstream labor and left-wing
political parties, so it appears that his work will be read and
understood (if that is possible) by only a few students. The im-
plication is that his life-long work will not have the impact on
the world that he had planned and that it has been only an egoistic achievement.

Perhaps the greatest benefits from Crimond's book are
the restoration of Gerard's creativity and the fruition of the
relationship between Gerard and Rose. However the later is

debatable since Rose, an intellectual in her own right, has wasted her life waiting for Gerard, and he finally realizes he needs her only as a research assistant. Gerard plans to write a book answering Crimond's book, point by point (pp. 571–72). It will be a long book, and he asks Rose to live with him and be his research assistant. The cycle may even begin anew because Gerard wants his book to represent the present views of the old circle of Oxford friends.

### The Message to the Planet (1989)

With *The Message to the Planet,* Iris Murdoch continues her ruminations on religion and the importance of being good. The concept of religion is considered through the cult figure Marcus Vallar, a Sephardic Jew. Like David Crimond from *The Book and the Brotherhood,* Vallar is an intellectual demon figure with an alternative vision of life. A brilliant mathematician, he had discovered at age nineteen "something amazing called the Vallar Theorem which shook the mathematical world and interested astrophysicists."[13] But after a few years Vallar lost interest in mathematics and began experimenting with other arts. He tried painting but abandoned it when he thought he had accomplished all it offered. In an effort to free himself of attachments which distracted him from his work, Vallar "engineered quarrels wherein he denounced" his friends (p. 15).[14] He left for California, where he joined a religious group that combined meditation with extraordinary physical feats (p. 16),[15] and then went on to the Far East, where he hoped to discover a unity principle for the universe.

Two of the friends whom Vallar denounced, Gildas Herne and Patrick Fenman, were harmed by his actions. Gildas had been a priest, and when Marcus pointed out that he should leave the priesthood since he did not have the faith he professed, Gildas did so. Patrick, a superstitious, failed Irish poet, was convinced that Marcus had cursed him during a quarrel, believed he would die from the curse, and eventually lapsed into a coma. In an effort to save Patrick, and also because he has an interest in Vallar's vision, the historian Alfred Ludens uncovers Marcus's whereabouts and asks him to revoke the curse. Marcus, who has been living in seclusion in the English countryside, now appears aged, infirm, and not quite sane, but he agrees to try to help Patrick. To effect this cure, Marcus "eased himself down so that he was partly lying on Patrick" and breathed slowly into Patrick's mouth (p. 127). After a while, he took his curse back: "Patrick, it's Marcus. Any ill thing I said to you I now take back, any harm I meant to you I hereby revoke. I ask you to pardon me. I command you to get well" (p. 129).

Patrick's recovery gains Marcus a reputation as a healer, and Ludens encourages him to formulate his thoughts and to write them down: "Now you've been following the way and you've discovered what you were looking for all those years, and now you've got to *clarify* that discovery, you've got to go *on*" (p. 316). But Marcus's daughter, Irina, believes Marcus has no message to give: "You are encouraging him, you're making him feel he's a great man with a message and it's do or die. Whereas really he's a helpless solitary person with a thoroughly confused mind'' (p. 196).

Although Irina then takes her father to Bellmain sanitarium for rest, his status as a religious figure continues to grow. Bellmain has a sarsen on its grounds, a great stone called the Axle Stone. A legend surrounding the stone claims that it was supposed to have been one of the Avebury Stones associated with a fertility cult (p. 240). These stones are thought to appear near centers of energy and are thought to be capable of moving about at midsummer (p. 241).

While at Bellmain, Ludens and Marcus sit on the oval concrete base of the stone, and Ludens questions Marcus, trying to help clarify his thoughts through a dialectic (p. 242). A Bellmain psychiatrist, Dr. Marzillian, who provides a coherent assessment of Marcus's powers and abilities, claims: ''It seems that he wants to solve a philosophical problem about the nature of human consciousness. He also envisages some duty or enactment which is to benefit mankind'' (p. 262).

Marcus's association with dialectic, the intellectual exercise which Plato felt could lead towards knowledge of the good (perfection), and his close proximity to the sarsen suggest an energy of ancient and primitive significance. Members of a cult called the Stone People think Marcus has special powers, and one young member, Fanny Amherst, leaves propitiatory offerings for Marcus at the base of the stone: ''wild flowers, laid down carefully, the flowers slightly separated'' (p. 278); later, flowers and pebbles appear, arranged in patterns (p. 283). She explains the Stone People's creed to Lu-

## LATEST WORKS (1983–1989)

dens: "It's all together, everything like that *must* be, because there are holy rays everywhere, these forces that gather into Holy Places, and into Holy Things like the Great Stones" (p. 328). Fanny believes that these rays are also gathered in some people and that Marcus may be such a holy person. Soon other young people appear, inquiring about "the place of healing" (p. 279) and wanting to see Marcus.

In addition to the Stone People, various open-minded religious figures recognize Marcus as possessing exceptional spiritual powers. Father O'Harte, an eccentric priest who had witnessed Patrick Fenman's return "from the dead," arrives at the sanitarium to observe Vallar; Rabbi Daniel Most views Vallar as a "conscience . . . to preserve the memory of what evil is and good is" (p. 417); Mr. Richard Talgarth, a Christian pastor, sees Vallar in the role of sadhu (p. 484), or mendicant ascetic, and says this phenomenon is unusual in England but would not be in India: "In that country there are gods everywhere. . . . They live with a concept of holiness which has vanished from the West" (p. 355). Such an ecclectic and eccumenical endorsement also attests to the possibility of religious universality.

At first Marcus accepts his role, allowing people to observe him and even holding sessions and giving advice. But he finds the pressure of being a savior for humanity enormously difficult and tells the onlookers that he cannot help them. Much like the Jews' reaction against Christ for not being the military savior whom they expected, the people gathered at Bellmain turn against Vallar and begin to stone him with the offerings which they have brought (p. 384).

## UNDERSTANDING IRIS MURDOCH

This view of spirituality as a seductive agent which may degenerate into a dangerous form of magic (healing) is a topic which has occurred elsewhere in Murdoch's canon, particularly in *The Sea, The Sea*, in which James Arrowby's paranormal powers detract from his spiritual amelioration. Several characters in *The Message to the Planet* comment on this possibility for Vallar. According to Gildas Herne, "He's a lost soul. He is sunk in the magic into which religion degenerates, what he wants is a spiritual power which has nothing to do with goodness. He wants to live forever. He probably will. He thinks he's God" (p. 45). Dr. Marzillian also refers to Marcus as a magician:

> He wanted to be a good magician. He had discovered that he had magical powers, paranormal powers as people say. But is there such a thing? What mortal can have such power and not be corrupted? . . . Having conjured up and used these powers, let the demons out . . . and having then opted for—let us say for the moment something higher—he might be overwhelmed by forces which were still his own, but now alien and hostile. (p. 497)

Following Marcus's death, Ludens says that Marcus was "destroyed by his own magic" (p. 497).

Marcus dies during the Midsummer Day ritual while the Seekers are gathered together and singing and chanting at the Axle Stone (pp. 463–65). Ludens, who had experienced an epiphany of understanding at the ritual, discovers Marcus with his head inside the gas oven and a prayer shawl draped over a nearby kitchen chair (p. 468). Although Ludens concludes that Marcus has committed suicide, there is better evidence for a willed death. Dr. Bland doesn't think Marcus has gassed himself because the kitchen is too well ventilated, and Marcus's appearance is not that of one who has died from asphyxiation. The death certificate (like James Arrowby's after his willed death) specifies that Marcus died from a sudden heart attack (p. 492). Dr. Marzillian calls the death unusual and feels that Marcus "enacted a psychological experience which killed him" (p. 496): "He once said that there could be such a death which would be significant, a sort of act of salvation, but one would have to be worthy of it" (p. 496).

Other reactions to Marcus's death suggest that he has done something beneficial for mankind. Rabbi Most thinks Marcus has died for the suffering of the world. Apparently the gas was symbolic of his acceptance of the sufferings of the Holocaust victims (p. 496). Patrick, too, believes Marcus is a martyr: "He died for me, instead of me, he took my illness when he took back the curse into himself. . . . He is for me Christ crucified" (p. 475). And Fanny Amherst calls Marcus's death a "salvation" (p. 505). But Dr. Marzillian gives a more moderate explanation of Marcus's powers to Ludens: "Your friend was an exceptional man, possessed of an outstanding intellect, and also surrounded by, indeed full of, forces which he did not entirely understand" (p. 496–97).

In many ways Marcus becomes whatever his followers need. Their willingness to accept him as a vicarious victim attests to the spiritual void which Iris Murdoch believes exists in the modern consciousness. And their grasping at a new universal spirituality reminds the reader of a similar response given by Father Jacoby in *The Philosopher's Pupil* when he claims that people must "hang on . . . until religion can change itself into something we can believe in" (p. 187). Marcus himself had expressed the need for a different view of God: "Well—perhaps we need a new god—not a maimed monster—as any human must become—We need after the Holocaust, a God that is no god" (p. 165). Rabbi Most realizes the importance of holding on to faith: "Nothing could be more important to this planet than preserving the name of God, we must not abandon it, it is entrusted to us in this age, to carry it onward through the darkness" (p. 417). This "darkness" signifies the modern lack of faith. The consideration of alternative visions of God and spirituality is an attempt to keep faith viable.

Alfred Ludens, who had really not believed that Marcus had any paranormal powers, became convinced that Marcus's genius could convey a message of universal understanding after he listened to a tape which Dr. Marzillian had made of Marcus speaking an unrecognizable language: "Perhaps he discovered it after all . . . the formula, the *message to the planet*, the universal understanding" (p. 508). Because suffering "is a universal condition . . . a sort of language" which we all experience but whose meaning "lies beyond us" (p. 509), Ludens feels that Marcus's suffering may be the message to the planet. However, while Marcus Vallar may have recorded a message of "universal understanding," he was unable to convey it in a manner which could be understood by others. Until such time as intimations of universal truths are grasped by the majority, Alfred Ludens must supply the message to the planet: "One must try to be good—just for nothing" (p. 437). For he indicates a means for moral improvement, which, for Murdoch, leads one toward truth. His response is, in fact, the same as one Murdoch gave when she was asked about the message she was trying to convey in this work: "The message is—everything is contingent. There are no deep foundations. Our life rests on chaos and rubble, and all we can try to do is be good."[16]

## *Notes*

1. For the past ten years Iris Murdoch has also been working on a philosophy manuscript (based on the Gifford Lectures), *Metaphysics as a Guide to Morals*, which was published by Chatto & Windus in 1992.

2. A Marxist in her youth, Murdoch soon became disenchanted with that system. She tells Jeffrey Meyers that *The Book and the Brotherhood* "came out of an interest in Marxism and the way in which people's ideas changed, out of having a lot of friends at the university." Meyers, "An Interview with Iris Murdoch," *Denver Quarterly* 26, no. 1 (Summer 1991): 108.

3. Iris Murdoch, *The Philosopher's Pupil* (New York: Viking Press, 1983), p. 89; subsequent references to this work are noted parenthetically in the text.

4. The German philosopher Moritz Schlick was murdered by one of his students. George McCaffrey makes a reference to this historical figure and perhaps contemplates the same relationship between himself and Rozanov, for he says, "I never did find out how Schlick's pupil killed him" (p. 556).

5. Iris Murdoch, *The Fire and the Sun: Why Plato Banished the Artists* (Oxford: Oxford University Press, 1977), p. 84.

6. Iris Murdoch explains her views on religion and claims to be a "Christian Buddhist" in the interview with Jeffrey Meyers, p. 110.

7. The dialectic between Father Jacoby and John Robert Rozanov takes place in *The Philosopher's Pupil* on pages 185–98.

8. Irene Simon, "A Note on Iris Murdoch's *The Good Apprentice*," *English Studies* 68, no. 1 (February 1987): 75–78. Irene Simon believes Edward Baltram is the good apprentice and that Stuart is not a prodigal son. Fernand Corin, "Rites of Passage in Iris Murdoch's *The Good Apprentice*," in *Multiple Worlds, Multiple Words*, ed. Henna Maes-Jelinek (Liège: University of Liège, 1988). Corin believes that both brothers are apprentices to goodness (p. 17).

9. Iris Murdoch, *The Good Apprentice* (New York: Viking Press, 1985), p. 24; subsequent references to this work are noted parenthetically in the text.

10. Meyers, p. 108.

11. Iris Murdoch, *The Book and the Brotherhood* (New York: Viking Press, 1988), p. 77; subsequent references to this work are noted parenthetically in the text.

12. See also Max Lejour in *The Unicorn* and John Robert Rozanov in *The Philosopher's Pupil*.

13. Iris Murdoch, *The Message to the Planet* (New York: Viking Press, 1989), p. 7; subsequent references to this work are noted parenthetically in the text.

14. His intentions are similar to those of John Robert Rozanov (*The Philosopher's Pupil*), who wanted no distractions to keep him from his great work.

15. Marcus Vallar is similar to James Arrowby (*The Sea, The Sea*), who had Tibetan powers of concentration which degenerated into magic.

16. Linda Wertheimer, *All Things Considered*, National Public Radio (New York City studios), broadcast February 26, 1990.

# CHAPTER SEVEN

# Other Novels and Plays

### *The Sandcastle* (1957)

$B$ecause of its popular appeal and romantic story line, *The Sandcastle* has never been considered by critics to be one of Murdoch's more successful works; nevertheless, it makes important statements concerning moral philosophy and aesthetics which are central to an understanding of the author's vision. In the area of moral philosophy, *The Sandcastle* introduces one of Murdoch's few good characters, Bledyard, an art master who demonstrates the connection between truth and moral virtue: those who perceive truth will act correctly. Bledyard also expresses the Platonic concern about the dangers inherent in representational art forms, discussed at length in *The Fire and the Sun: Why Plato Banished the Artists.*

The plot of *The Sandcastle* involves a May-December romance between Bill Mor, a teacher at St. Bride's school, and a young painter, the sprite-like Rain Carter, who has been commissioned to paint a portrait of St. Bride's former headmaster, Demoyte. The moral complications for the couple involve Mor's wife, Nan, and his teenage children, Donald and Felicity.

Bledyard realizes the interconnectedness of all things and is able to make accurate moral judgments. When Mor contemplates deserting his wife and children for Rain, Bledyard senses the situation and points out the damaging effects which such an action would have, not only on Mor's family, but also on Rain's ability to paint: "You are diminishing her by involving her in this. A painter can only paint what he is. You will prevent her from being a great painter."[1] Indeed, Rain recognizes that her portrait of Demoyte is less than good and is able to repaint and improve the head after she breaks off with Mor: "I must finish this. I want to repaint the head. I see what to do now. I must go on working" (p. 330).

Because Bledyard is a man with "total disregard of convention" (p. 75) and deeply concerned with the welfare of others, he speaks his mind on almost any issue. The things he says to Rain and to Mor upset them very much. "When we look upon a human face, we interpret it by what we are ourselves," Bledyard tells Rain (p. 81). These views on representative art make Rain feel that "everything she does [in art] must be rotten" (p. 86). Bledyard also confronts Mor about his behavior: "The point is not to lament or cry out *mea maxima culpa,* but rather to do the thing that is right" (p. 230). Yet for all their uneasiness with him, both Rain and Mor value Bledyard's good opinion (pp. 182, 173). And when Mor's son Donald, and Donald's friend Carde become trapped while climbing the school's tower, Bledyard figures calmly and effectively in Donald's rescue from the building's parapet after Carde's fall (pp. 276–92). The reader thus perceives Bledyard as capable of decisive and correct action and not merely as a moralizer.

### *A Severed Head* (1961)

A witty, ironical, and satirical novel, *A Severed Head* presents a comedy of manners which includes the pairing and switching of partners in almost every conceivable situation among its small cast of characters. The novel is a delightful satire of Freudian theory, so much so that some have felt it necessary to defend psychoanalysis from implications made in the novel.[2] When the story opens, Martin Lynch-Gibbon and his considerably younger mistress, Georgie Hands, discuss their certainty that Martin's wife, Antonia, is ignorant of their affair. As the egoist narrator, Lynch-Gibbon assures the reader of his powerful position in his marriage: "In almost every marriage there is a selfish and an unselfish partner. . . . In my own marriage I early established myself as the one who took rather than gave."[3] He returns home from Georgie's rooms on the day of Antonia's regular appointment with her American psychoanalyst, Palmer Anderson, quite pleased with himself and his situation, believing himself "the luckiest of men" (p. 24). Ironically, when Antonia arrives home, she pours him a large drink and announces that she wants a divorce so that she can marry Anderson (p. 27).

In his efforts to take what he considers to be a civilized stand on the matter, Martin finds himself buffeted by love and jealously as he and the other characters parade through one another's arms. Furthering the Freudian themes, it appears that Martin may have initially fallen in love with Antonia, a woman considerably older than he is, because she is a mother figure. And after Antonia's announcement, Antonia and Palmer advise Martin much as parents would. In an extended case of sibling rivalry, Martin keeps Georgie away from his brother, Alexander, because he used to take all of his girls away from him. Once Antonia and Martin separate, Martin backs away from marrying Georgie and admits that he would like to keep her in cold storage (p. 145). However, his interest is aroused once again when he finds his brother visiting her. And his old love for Georgie is rekindled by a telephone call from his brother announcing his plans to marry Georgie: "With a hideous rush, like blood returning to a crushed limb, I was invaded by my old love for Georgie; and in that instant I realized how very much I had all the same, all the same, all the same, relied upon her faithfulness" (p. 190).

The absence of children in the novel advances a theme of sterility. Antonia appears to have been unable to conceive, but Georgie has an abortion when she discovers herself pregnant with Martin's child. The abortion remains as a source of grief, especially to Georgie, and Martin's inadvertent mention of the topic of children devastates both women (pp. 196–97). This want of children appears to instigate the characters' parental behavior toward one another and, perhaps, their childish behavior.

## OTHER NOVELS AND PLAYS

Although Martin tries to maintain a civil relationship with Antonia and Palmer, he finds himself reacting more to the loss of his friendship with Palmer than to the dissolution of his marriage to Antonia. When he serves the couple wine in bed, Martin is "troubled by Palmer's naked body under the silk robe" (p. 129). He is troubled once again by the proximity of Palmer's naked body after discovering him in an incestuous relationship with his half sister, Honor Klein (p. 155).

Martin is also attracted to Honor Klein, feeling a love for her which may have been strengthened by his seeing her in bed with her half brother. Honor believes this love may have subconscious origins, perhaps having to do with the myth of Candaules and Gyges: "Candaules was proud of the beauty of his wife and he wanted his friend Gyges to see her naked. He concealed Gyges in the bedroom—but Candaules' wife realized that he was there. Then later, because he had seen her, she approached him and forced him to kill Candaules and become king himself" (pp. 247–48). But other myths are intertwined in the story. Honor Klein, initially described as repulsive and ugly, has dark locks and eyes resembling those of the Gorgon Medusa, who had living snakes for hair and whose head was severed by the hero Perseus. When Martin reveals his love for Honor, he observes, "She simply stared at me and I saw the old snake in her looking coldly out through her eyes" (p. 218). Another reason for Martin's attraction to Honor explains the novel's title: "Because of what I am and because of what you saw I am a terrible object of fascination for you. I am a severed head such as primitive tribes and old alchemists used to use, anointing it with oil and putting a morsel of gold upon its tongue to make it utter prophecies'' (p. 221).

The other characters also suffer from jealousy, and each startling revelation lends wit and irony to this fast-paced plot. It seems that the sibling rivalry was justified, for Antonia began an affair with Alexander before she married Martin. Alexander's engagement to Georgie, according to Antonia, was revenge for her having decided to marry Anderson (p. 230). Once that marriage is off, Antonia and Alexander decide to marry each other. In a final comic touch, the psychoanalyst, who should have been least shocked by these revelations, is the most desperate to escape from the situation. Honor tells Martin that Georgie and Palmer have gone away to America for good and that she will remain in England: ''Palmer and Georgie became very fond of each other. . . . I don't know what they'll make of it. But Palmer wanted to get away, he was frantic to get away'' (p. 247).

The denouement of the novel does not necessarily suggest a happy union between Honor Klein and Martin Lynch-Gibbon. Honor, an anthropologist, appears an alien and dark power figure and is seen throughout the novel with the accompaniment of pervasive fog. She has studied the samurai sword in Japan, where ''the use of them is not merely an art but a spiritual exercise'' (p. 116). She reminds Martin, ''Being a Christian, you connect spirit with love. These people connect it with control, with power'' (p. 116). And Martin seems to recognize danger in their attraction: '' 'I haven't come *to* torment you,' said Honor. She was serious, but there was an ironical lightness in her gaze. 'Of course, I understand it may

## OTHER NOVELS AND PLAYS

happen inadvertently,' I said. 'I know you have the temperament of an assassin' '' (p. 247).

### *A Severed Head* (play) (1964)

The most successful stage adaptation of Iris Murdoch's novels, *A Severed Head,* resulted from a collaboration between Murdoch and J. B. Priestley. The play, a popular success, had ''a provincial try-out at the Theatre Royal, Bristol, on 7 May [1963],'' and then ran ''for two and a half years at the [London] Criterion.''[4] It also ran for about three weeks at the Royale Theatre in New York.[5] In 1964 Chatto & Windus published a reading edition, *A Severed Head: A Play in Three Acts,* which is described as ''an expanded version of the text used at the Criterion Theatre.''[6] The acting edition, also published in 1964 by Samuel French, followed the 1963 Donald Albery production at the Criterion. Further testimony to the play's success are the Samuel French reissue (1967), and Italian (1965), German (1966), and Japanese (1967) editions.[7] The play was also performed in the Netherlands in a Dutch translation,[8] and a motion picture based on the novel and the play was released by Columbia Pictures in 1971.

Some of the reasons for its success, according to John Fletcher, are that it ''has all the speed, elaboration and stylisation of a Restoration comedy, and develops an action which, if not particularly credible, never fails to sustain the audience's interest and involvement.''[9] But while the main changes in the acting version of the novel involve alterations for brevity, some of the cuts also affect the meaning of the play. According to Fletcher, the character of Georgie seems silly and not fully realized, and the sterility theme is significantly altered when her abortion is omitted.[10]

## The Red and the Green (1965)

*The Red and the Green,* Iris Murdoch's only historical novel, concerns the Easter Rebellion in support of Home Rule which took place in Dublin in April 1916. Sinn Feiners, Irish nationalists, took over the Dublin Post Office and replaced the British Union Jack with a green flag "with the words *Irish Republic* written upon it in white letters."[11]

The novel's themes, sexual initiation and obsession with religion and past, are similar to the prominent themes of James Joyce's *Dubliners.* The main theme of initiation is shown through Andrew Chase-White. Barnabas Drumm, a promising medieval scholar and failed priest, is rendered impotent by conflicting demands of celibacy and religious scruples. And all of the characters are affected by the question of Irish nationalism, whether they support it or not. Hilda Chase-White, Andrew's mother, illustrates the Irish obsession with history: "Why do people in Ireland always talk about *history*? . . . My head's always swimming with dates when I'm over here. English people don't talk about English history all the time" (p. 37).

An Anglo-Irish officer, Andrew Chase-White has been commissioned in King Edward's Horse and is in Ireland on

## OTHER NOVELS AND PLAYS

leave before going to the front during World War I. Andrew has proposed to an Irish girl, Frances Bellman; however, she refuses his proposal because she is secretly in love with Andrew's cousin, Pat Dumay, a nationalist who is killed during the Easter Rising.

Andrew's confusion over his loyalties is expressed early in the novel: "Andrew had grown up in England and more especially in London, and felt himself unreflectively to be English, although equally unreflectively he normally announced himself as Irish" (pp. 4–5). Andrew feels inferior and insecure around his Irish cousins, not only because they are superior in sports and games (p. 15) but because they seem to have a clear direction about their loyalties.

Many of these relatives are Irish nationalists, and the topic of nationalism is debated throughout the novel, particularly through the characters of Frances's father, Christopher Bellman, and Andrew's cousins, Cathal and Pat Dumay. Bellman, an Irish "enthusiast," is an expert on the antiquities of Ireland and familiar with Gaelic (pp. 23, 24). Pat Dumay had an "early sense of his Irish destiny, his sense of belonging not to himself but to some design of history" (p. 80); he is killed in the fighting on the Thursday of Easter week, the day before the nationalists surrendered (p. 310). His brother, Cathal, an ardent nationalist, reportedly joins the Irish Republican Army and is killed in the Irish civil war in 1921 (p. 310). By contrast, Andrew is both frightened of going to war and uncertain of his loyalties.

Although the framework for the novel concerns the Easter Rising, the novel itself details the confusion and insecurity which accompany Andrew Chase-White's sexual initiation, which was intertwined in his mind with the idea of his death (p. 21). The novel also details the destruction of his honor as a British officer, which Andrew surrenders when he is blackmailed into agreeing not to reveal the plans for the Irish uprising to the British. His aunt, Millie Kinnard, had threatened to tell Andrew's mother about an incestuous relationship which Millie had had with her half brother, Andrew's father, unless Andrew cooperated with the Irish nationalists.

In many ways this treatment of the question of Irish nationalism appears sentimental, for the historical figures associated with this rebellion have become Irish folk heroes. And although historical events portrayed in *The Red and the Green* are tragic, the characters are seen as zealots and idealists and appeared heroic when the novel was published in 1965. Even though she is Anglo-Irish, Iris Murdoch says she finds it difficult to write about Ireland today because the current troubles are too terrible.[12]

### *The Servants and the Snow* (1970)

The first play which Murdoch wrote directly for the stage rather than as an adaptation of a novel, *The Servants and the Snow* premiered on September 29, 1970, at the Greenwich Theatre, London.[13] Its main theme is the abuse of power; the victims of power then misuse power themselves. In a related theme, the weak position of women is considered through such remarks as one made by the servant Marina who is be-

## OTHER NOVELS AND PLAYS

trothed to another servant, Peter Jack: "A married woman is a slave. Men are all the same. You are kind to me now. But once we were married you wouldn't value me any more. And you'd be violent in the end. All men are violent in the end."[14] Another prominent issue is the decay of Christianity, shown through the "enlightened" humanism of Basil and his wife and by Father Ambrose, an old priest who tells Basil that they will not be needing a new church: "I shall have no successor here. When I die, which please God will be soon, these people will revert to a paganism which is very much more natural to them than the religion which I have preached and failed to practice" (p. 59).

Basil is the well-intentioned master of an isolated country estate inherited from his cruel father, who had ruled the household as a feudal lord and used fear to maintain order among his two hundred servants. Basil's father has committed such atrocities as shooting gypsies for sport, murdering the husband of a servant girl whom he intended to take as a mistress, and claiming the droit du seigneur, the supposed right to have sexual relations with the local brides on their wedding nights. Now, although Basil wants to establish democracy, the secrets of the past cast gloom upon the present. It is revealed that Basil's father has been murdered by Father Ambrose, who warns Basil not to attempt to make restitution for his father's deeds because the servants, as victims of power, respect only power. They will see Basil's attempts to change the archaic practices as a sign of weakness. Consequently he is in danger of becoming involved in a blood feud: "A blood feud is not easily ended here, and you are your father's son. There are very deep compulsions, primitive ideas of justice which are still alive in this place, perhaps because of the long dark winter times, perhaps because of the snow'' (p. 73). When Basil then reverses his democratic stand, thinking that the droit du seigneur with Marina can become a source of redemptive love, his wife, Oriane, murders him for this humiliation. Following Basil's murder, the play ends with the entrance of Oriane's brother, the authoritarian General Klein, who takes charge of the situation by harshly ordering the servants about and referring to them as swine (p. 112). It is clear to the reader that he will restore order by resorting to the tactics of fear used by Basil's father.

### *An Accidental Man* (1971)

*An Accidental Man* contains several of Murdoch's least palpable characters and offers little hope for their redemption. While the motifs common to Murdoch novels—power, pain, guilt, alienation, suffering, redemption, and forgiveness—are again present, the contingencies of life and lack of redemptive characters present a horrific life vision. There has been debate about the identification of the title character. Peter Conradi notes that American critics usually ascribe Ludwig Leferrier this position because he is an American,[15] although it could also be pointed out that he is the novel's one redemptive character. Other critics view Austin Gibson Grey as the accidental man, and he actually identifies himself as such.[16]

In discussing her method of invention, Murdoch remarked that the kernel of the story which began *An Accidental*

## OTHER NOVELS AND PLAYS

*Man* was an automobile accident, in which Austin Gibson Grey, who had been drinking, ran over a six-year-old girl, Rosalind Monkley, and tried to persuade his brother, Matthew, to say he had been driving the car.[17] The almost existential contingency surrounding the accident and the mother's anguished grief, which separates her from those who have not had this experience, make the reader aware of the accidental nature of life.

Austin Gibson Grey, is described as "a huge fat egoist, as fat as a bull-frog" (p. 294). His life exemplifies the contingency of the world, for he has been fired without a pension and appears to have been unlucky with his wives. His first, Betty, drowned (or was murdered by a jealous Austin) and his second, Dorina, is electrocuted in the bath. For Austin, "life was misery and muddle, it *was* misery and muddle" (p. 111).

Austin feels himself a victim of life, and his hand is literally paralyzed by the jealousy he feels for Matthew. Austin's reaction to insecurity always includes violence: he probably killed his first wife, Betty, because he believed she was having an affair with Matthew; he bashed the head of Norman Monkley, the stepfather of the girl he killed, when Norman tried to blackmail him (p. 245); he killed an owl with a brick when it flew at him (p. 283); and he smashed Matthew's priceless porcelain collection in yet another jealous rage (p. 343). Austin keeps the fey and innocent Dorina "almost literally cloistered" at Valmorana with her sister, Mavis (p. 60). And he appears relieved at Dorina's death: "He had wanted Dorina to be held prisoner from the world, to be held secure for him. Now she was shut up forever in the most final of all prisons. Now at least she was absolutely safe, and could never hurt him anymore" (pp. 368–69).

The object of much of Austin's rivalry and hatred is his
brother, "a horribly successful diplomat" (p. 13) who returns
to London from Japan on a quest to make peace with Austin:
"It was ironic that the great task of his retirement seemed to
be simply to cure his younger brother of a crippling hatred"
(p. 123). But Matthew, like Murdoch's other collectors, also
has a hunger for power. Charlotte Ledgard tells him: "You set
up in business as a sort of sage. . . . You want power where
it's interesting" (p. 379). And when Austin finally frees himself from his emotional tangle with Matthew, Matthew almost
appears disappointed:

> I came to set him free, thought Matthew. I came to
> change magic into spirit. It was all to be brought
> about by me. Now when it appears that somehow or
> other, by means which I do not even understand, he
> has got out, I ought to be glad . . . I wanted that bond
> to be cut, but I did want to cut it myself. (pp. 411–12)

Austin's son, Garth, graduated from Cambridge and
studied philosophy at Harvard. An absolutist with existential
leanings, Garth had been concerned with freedom, correct
choice, and action but gave up philosophy because he felt it
had no meaning in his life. He had witnessed a murder on the
streets of New York, did not try to interfere, and felt no guilt
for this failure to act. Garth recorded his experience in a novel,
which he describes as a "false sort of thing—personal muck"
(p. 106). The hero's suicide coincides with Garth's own spiritual death; since he cannot endure the contingent conditions
relative to life, Garth prefers capitulation to spiritual imper-

fection: "The contingent details of choice disturbed him. Everything that was offered him was too particular, too hole and corner and accidental, not significant enough, though at the same time he realized with dazzling clarity that all decent things which human beings do are hole and corner" (p. 161). However, his friend Ludwig Leferrier is not impressed by Garth's position:

> This sense of Garth's pointlessness was increased for
> Ludwig by Garth's own gloom. . . . But someone like
> Garth had no right to be depressed. At Harvard he
> had spoken with glittering eyes of the freedom which
> comes to the truly destitute. There was no air of tri-
> umph now. . . . There is a great force in him, thought
> Ludwig, a great fire, but all the same he will waste
> himself. (p. 200)

Ludwig's remarks seem prophetic, for Garth grasps for wealth and "happiness" by marrying the wealthy Gracie Tisbourne.

Ludwig, an American student living in London and avoiding the Vietnam draft because he was born in England, also has a moral dilemma. He is faced with the choice of fulfilling his dreams by taking up his Oxford appointment and marrying the girl he loves, Gracie Tisbourne, or returning to America to face charges of draft evasion. Ludwig had studied philosophy with Garth at Harvard. Unlike Garth, Ludwig maintains his idealism, returns to America, and is imprisoned.

Many of the characters in *An Accidental Man* fit the Peter Pan motif because they are spiritually immature and unwilling to grow up and account for themselves.[18] But the novel contains an especially comic treatment of the motif when plump and stodgy Sir Matthew Gibson Grey dashes across Hyde Park in an effort to avoid listening to Gracie Tisbourne's problems. The "jog," ending beside the Peter Pan statue in Kensington Gardens, leaves Matthew breathless, exhausted, and prey to Gracie's intrusion anyway, for she effortlessly catches up with him. Matthew, described by his nephew as capable of listening to other people's life stories and then promptly forgetting them, and the materialistic Gracie Tisbourne carefully assess each other while the reader, recognizing them as two of the novel's most self-adsorbed characters, notes the ironic significance of their conducting this activity in close proximity to the statue of Peter Pan.

### *The Three Arrows* (1972)

Like *The Servants and the Snow, The Three Arrows* was written directly for the stage rather than adapted from a novel. It was first performed on October 17, 1972, at the Arts Theatre Cambridge, with Ian McKellen in the lead. It is a two-act political drama set in medieval Japan, with a curious mix of Irish accents, English phrasings, and a Shakespearean restoration of order in the last scene.[19] Iris Murdoch identifies its major themes as "the nature of power and sovereignty . . . freedom versus the hierarchal system."[20]

The lead character, Prince Yorimitsu, led a peasant rebellion and has been imprisoned for five years in the imperial palace, kept alive by a balance of power between the shogun, General Musashi, and the imperial family, who are afraid to move against him because of his popular support. Tokuzan, the ex-emperor who is now a monk, continues as the power behind the throne of Taihito, the young emperor. Tokuzan suggests that Yorimitsu marry Keiko, the crown princess, in an effort to ally him with the imperial family. Marriage to the crown princess requires a traditional ordeal of the three arrows; if the suitor chooses wrong, he must commit seppuku. The arrows, representing love, action, and holiness, are appropriate for Prince Yorimitsu because he loves the crown princess, is writing a treatise on political economy, and has considered entering the monastery. The ceremony has been rigged by Prince Tenjiku so that the arrow flares red, signifying Yorimitsu's death. However, the young emperor then cites precedent for a second ordeal whereby Yorimitsu may choose love (but remain a prisoner), freedom (but without his love), or honor (death by seppuku). Prince Yorimitsu chooses freedom.

In a tragic restoration of order, the prince is released to join his troops in the north; the shogun is mistakenly killed by Okano, Yorimitsu's samurai, while trying to save Yorimitsu from Tenjiku's men at the ordeal; Tenjiku is arrested by the young emperor's men, and Keiko quietly kills herself within her litter. It is unclear whether she has committed suicide because she thought Yorimitsu would die or because he chose freedom.

### *The Sacred and Profane Love Machine* (1974)

Like *The Nice and the Good, The Sacred and Profane Love Machine* recalls a painting which illustrates the dual nature of love. Here the title of Titian's painting *Sacred and Profane Love,* concerns both divine and human love.[21] This duality is best illustrated through Blaise Gavender, an unqualified psychotherapist with a penchant for dream interpretation, whose wife, Harriet (described as a near-saint and developed as a nearly good figure), and his mistress, Emily McHugh (whose appeal for Blaise appears to be primarily erotic), fulfill these roles. Blaise's situation, having a wife and son in the country and a mistress and son in the city, prompts him to suggest a ménage à trois, a situation which recurs in other Murdoch novels.[22] Blaise's wife and son David live in a suburban Victorian house with a garden, and his mistress and autistic son Luca live a mean existence in a Putney flat. When Luca stows away in Blaise's car and appears in the garden at Hood House, Blaise decides to reveal his double life to his wife. Once his second family is made known, Emily pressures Blaise to live with them and support them. Because Blaise does not have the courage to tell Harriet of his decision to live with Emily, he informs her by letter and asks her to keep the household going for him.

In many ways Harriet Gavender resembles a saint, for she possesses humility and is confident of her ability to act correctly: "No . . . [one] could have been more confident than Harriet that she was a good person and would always be able to act rightly."[23] Her practice of collecting homeless dogs manifests Harriet's warmth and ability to love. She also takes the unwanted Luca and the depressed Monty Small, a neighbor, under her care and appears initially as a benevolent mother figure. But attributing goodness to Harriet seems to be a convenience for other characters, almost a license for their own solipsistic concerns, and Harriet is eventually overwhelmed by the burden of her husband's request to go on as usual. When her appeals to Blaise, Monty, and the fictitious Magnus Bowles (Monty's invention to cover Blaise's nights with Emily) prove disappointing, Harriet finally escapes from Hood House, taking Luca with her. En route to visit her brother in Hohne, she realizes her limited abilities:

> I am not the good person I used to think that I was. If I were forced to be their victim I could not do it with clear eyes and a humble, loving mind. I would do it with secret resentment and hatred. Not even that, for resentment and hatred are forms of strength. I would become weak and spiteful and demoralized and crazed with humiliation. I would writhe like a half-killed worm and would have no way of thinking about myself. (p. 339)

But in a final selfless act during a terrorist attack at Hanover airport, Harriet saves Luca's life by throwing herself on him, "shielding him with her bullet-riddled body" (p. 343).

Peter Conradi has called this novel a "black comedy about male vanity and female power,"[24] and indeed all of the men in the novel feel ensnared by women. Blaise's guilt for his adultery increases because of Harriet's goodness, and he wishes her out of his life. Emily's nagging also proves a burden to him until she achieves her goal, supplanting Harriet at Hood House. In lesser ways the denouement of the novel also involves the women's taking possession of the men. Kiki St.

Loy, described as "oversexed" and "rebellious" (p. 57), seduces Monty Small. Constance Pinn seduces Blaise's son David. And Edgar Demornay, the head of an Oxford college, who had been somewhat of a mother's boy and unsuccessful with women in youth, finds, to his joy, that three women are after him by the novel's close (p. 374).

Monty Small is particularly obsessed with and oppressed by the women in his life. Monty is supposedly in anguish over the death of his beloved wife, Sophie, but actually he strangled Sophie in order to avoid the prolonged suffering of watching her die from cancer. Monty's mother also has an obsessive love for him which had nearly suffocated him as a child. Now that her daughter-in-law is dead, Mrs. Small launches an aggressive effort to win her son back. Since he has silenced the telephone to avoid her calls, Léonie enters the novel through her love letters to Monty. But Monty appears quite capable of protecting himself, for when his mother arrives at the end of the novel she discovers that Monty has escaped to Italy (p. 372).

The novel addresses suffering as a form of consolation, both through Monty, who by his masochism "felt like a victim constantly revived in order to suffer more" (p. 112), and through Emily, who announces her unwillingness to continue suffering for Blaise (p. 86). But Harriet, who originally carries on at home through Blaise's unfaithfulness as a form of consolation, becomes a sacrificial victim, releasing Blaise from his dilemma and promoting Emily to a place at Hood House.

## OTHER NOVELS AND PLAYS

This denouement, less than morally satisfying, recalls the dark ending of *An Accidental Man.* Any optimism about the future, indicated by Emily's pregnancy, is also questionable, considering the fate of Blaise and Emily's first child, who is institutionalized at the end of the novel. Luca had been the object of so little love and communicated only with Harriet and animals. Now Blaise is relieved to be rid of him: "It was a relief to have it officially *classified* as subnormal and taken away to be looked after by experts" (p. 348). Even though the doctors are optimistic about his improvement, how could any child thrive without love?

### *A Word Child* (1975)

In one of Iris Murdoch's most detailed London settings, *A Word Child* demonstrates the maladjustment of those bereft of love. The narrator and title character, Hilary Burde, an emotionally abused orphan who has grown up feeling he was unlovable,[25] lives a maimed existence, repeating the mistakes of his past and being unable to love. Ironically, Hilary has highly developed linguistic skills, but they function mechanically and do not provide a basis for communion with others. In order to minimize human interaction, he carefully compartmentalizes his friends, visiting certain friends only on certain days of the week. This division becomes the framing structure of the novel, for all the chapters except the last two—which take place following Lady Kitty's death when there are "no more days'' (p. 377)—are entitled as days of the week. Hilary lives by rules, says Freddie Impiatt; "He separates everything from everything" (p. 8). As a further anonymity, he spends his spare time with strangers, riding beneath central London on the underground's Inner Circle line. Mechanical scheduling thus fills his life and precludes real human interaction. The main themes of the novel are the debilitating consequences of his failure to love (alienation and sterility), the importance of forgiving oneself and others for mistakes of the past, and the importance of spiritual redemption, all of which Hilary comes to realize during the course of the novel.

Through Hilary Burde, Murdoch develops the Peter Pan motif common in her novels.[26] Spiritually immature and self-absorbed, those characters associated with Peter Pan are reluctant to function responsibly in the adult world; Peter Pan also evokes negative connotations of childhood and parental relations. *A Word Child* presents a complex parent-child relationship between Hilary Burde and his Oxford tutor, Gunnar Jopling, who has been both friend and father figure to Hilary. Hilary had seduced Gunnar's first wife, Anne, and was culpable for her death and that of her unborn child and, indirectly, for the later suicide of Gunnar and Anne's son, who had once discovered Hilary and Anne in bed together. The tragedy not only maims Gunnar with hatred but also ruins Hilary's life; he leaves Oxford, accepts a mediocre civil service job, and withdraws from the world.

However, much like a little boy who continually wants what he cannot have and remains in competition with his father for his mother's love, Hilary also falls in love with Gunnar's second wife, Kitty, when twenty years later she asks him to help Gunnar dispel the ghosts of their past. Their meetings take place in Kensington Gardens, where the Peter Pan statue becomes their "place." The statue takes on connotations beyond their illicit relationship, entering into the unconscious darkness of Hilary's childhood fantasies. Hilary even imagines that Peter Pan listens to his conversation with Lady Kitty: "Behind [Kitty] upon his wet pedestal of beasts and fairies, polished and sanctified by the hands of children, towered beyond their reach the sinister boy, listening" (p. 197). It is just here, in the realm of childhood fantasy, fairies, and defiance, that Hilary falls in love with Lady Kitty.

Gunnar Jopling elaborates on the Peter Pan motif through his reaction to the news that *Peter Pan* will be the Whitehall office Christmas pantomime: "The fragmentation of spirit is the problem of our age. . . . Peter personifies a spirituality which is irrevocably caught in childhood and which yet cannot surrender its pretensions. Peter is essentially a being from elsewhere, the apotheosis of an immature spirituality" (p. 227). Gunnar's remarks make Hilary acutely uncomfortable, for they accurately portray his own situation.

Although neither Hilary nor Gunnar has been able to recover from the loss of Jopling's first wife and two children, Hilary repeats the mistakes of the past by falling in love with Kitty, who wants Hilary to give her a child to help Gunnar overcome his bitterness. Thus the retention of childhood and the loss of children are prominent themes in the novel. The theme of sterility is extended through Hilary's efforts to prevent his sister's marriage; his refusal to marry his former mistress, Tommy Uhlmeister; and the presence of a childless couple, Freddie and Laura Impiatt, who befriend Hilary.

Not only does the past repeat itself with the death of Gunnar's second wife, but we learn that both Hilary and Gunnar have been obsessed with the past: " 'You can perhaps have no idea,' Gunnar went on, 'how obsessed I have been with the past. Some people can get over tragedies in their lives. I have never managed to get over this one.' 'Neither have I,' I said. 'I have never stopped feeling guilty . . .' " (p. 263).

Hilary's childish and destructive behavior toward women is apparently driven by his fantasies about courtly love. He views himself as a quester in his relationship with Lady Kitty (p. 214), but, like other knights, he proves himself unworthy, and his connection with Lady Kitty causes her death. Further, Hilary's sister, Crystal, an uneducated, thirty-seven-year-old dressmaker, lives a lonely and wretched life in a small, shabby bed-sitter. And Hilary believes he is protecting his sister when he objects to her marriage to Arthur Mervyn Fisch, whom he describes as "a little untalented unambitious man, destined to spend his life in a cupboard" (p. 287), but he actually blocks her opportunity for happiness. Crystal finally asserts herself, sees Gunnar on the evening Hilary usually reserved for visiting her (p. 274), and marries Arthur Fisch on Christmas Eve.

Two other women treated badly by Hilary are Tommy Uhlmeister and Alexandra Bissett. Hilary would like to drop Tommy, his former mistress, but she lives a miserable existence waiting for him (p. 83). Alexandra Bissett (Biscuit), who is Lady Kitty's maid, acts as the courier between Lady Kitty and Hilary. Biscuit has invented a romantic background for

## OTHER NOVELS AND PLAYS

herself, but she is really the daughter of a waitress and an un-known Indian or Pakistani. Although Hilary felt akin to Bis-cuit because they "were both wanderers in society, both disinherited, both lost and both unclaimed" (p. 386), he did not return her love and viewed her as a serving girl.

Clifford Larr's suicide finally causes Hilary to realize that he has failed all of the people who have cared about him. Larr, a kind and eccentric homosexual, was a friend to Hilary but not his lover. Following the deaths of Kitty and Clifford, Hilary sits in St. Stephen's Church thinking about all of the people he has disappointed. He then realizes that Clifford "had died of being unloved and uncared for" (p. 380) and ex-periences real remorse for his own selfish life:

> And I wept, and gradually in the vagueness of misery,
> wept for Kitty, for Gunnar, for Anne and in some qui-eter way for myself. And after a while I began think-ing about Mr. Osmand, and how he had died alone,
> and how he had once taught me out of Kennedy's
> Latin Primer to conjugate the verb of love, his shabby
> coat sleeve pressing gently against my arm. (p. 380)

### *Henry and Cato* (1976)

One of this novel's title figures, Henry Marshalson, is an-other of Murdoch's characters who recognizes some truth through a mystical experience but finds it too horrific to em-brace and chooses instead to live a worldly and mediocre life.

## UNDERSTANDING IRIS MURDOCH

A failed artist, Henry left England for America (intending never to return) after obtaining a second-class degree in modern history at Cambridge.[27] He spent three years "messing with a doctorate" at Stanford (p. 4) and finally "obtained an insecure teaching post at a small liberal arts college at Sperriton, Illinois" (p. 4), passing himself off as an art historian. He has been working on a book about the painter Max Beckmann for nine years, but Henry believes he will probably not finish it (p. 134).[28]

As the novel opens, Henry is en route to England to claim his inheritance. He belongs to a family which practices primogeniture and had found out while he was in a bar in St. Louis that his elder brother had died. For Henry, "inheriting the property was nothing. What mattered was that bloody Sandy was no more" (p. 4). Henry resents bitterly the fact that Sandy was his mother's favorite son, and when he finds himself in possession of Laxlinden, the family estate, its monies, and the power over its distribution, he sets about making his mother as uncomfortable as possible by announcing his intention of breaking the property into small plots for a modern town.

Initially Henry displays no moral awareness; he has little concern for others, thinks consistently of his own whims and comforts, and acts in a selfish and destructive manner. However, through an episode which teaches him the meaning of fear and suffering (the subjects of Beckmann's paintings), he receives an opportunity for spiritual advancement. This incident also involves the other title character, Cato Forbes, Henry's childhood friend and a failed priest who lost his faith when he became enamored of a street thug, Beautiful Joe Beckett. Unfortunately, this same incident is also responsible for the spiritual destruction of Cato, who holds moral promise in the novel because his mentor is Brendan Craddock, one of Murdoch's few saints. Brendan, a Platonist whose pronouncements on enlightened and shadowed vision, love, death, suffering, and the use of power echo Murdoch's own beliefs, explains why Henry and Cato ultimately fail to maintain spiritual awareness:

> Death is what instructs us most of all, and then only when it is present. When it is absent it is totally forgotten. Those who can live with death can live in the truth, only this is almost unendurable. . . . Death is the great destroyer of all images and all stories, and human beings will do anything rather than envisage it. (p. 371)

The incident which causes Henry and Cato to reconsider their values involves kidnapping, betrayal, and homicide. When Beautiful Joe learns that Henry is wealthy, he kidnaps Cato and demands a ransom of twenty thousand pounds for his safe return. Henry's meeting with Beautiful Joe, who mutilates him for failing to bring the entire amount demanded, jolts Henry into an understanding of the darker side of existence. After this encounter, he realizes how drastically his life has changed: "Fear had entered his life and would now be with him forever" (p. 262). For the first time he feels an affinity with Max Beckmann and vicariously identifies with the suffering hero of one of Beckmann's pictures.

The terror escalates when Beckett forces Cato to ask his sister, Colette, to bring the next installment of the ransom. Beautiful Joe then imprisons Colette, paralyzing the actions of the three principal victims because they believe that Beautiful Joe is only one of an international terrorist gang from whom they will never be free. The kidnapping is finally resolved when Cato frees himself as Beautiful Joe attacks Colette; Cato hears her screams and clubs Beckett with a pipe, killing him. When Henry, Cato, and Colette learn that the kidnapping had been a one-man operation it is apparent that Cato has needlessly betrayed his sister and killed the boy whom he had loved.

Following a farewell meeting with Cato, at which it becomes clear that the ordeal has ruined Cato's life, Henry takes a cab to the National Gallery and sits in front of Titian's painting of Diana and Actaeon. His experiences with fear and suffering, both in his own and in Cato's life, have shown him something which he had failed to recognize during nine years of studying the paintings of an artist who depicted only fear and suffering. The representation of suffering in art does not begin to compare to actual suffering in real life:

> He stared at the picture and his heart became quiet. How different it is, violence in art, from the horror of the real thing. The dogs are tearing out Actaeon's entrails while the indifferent goddess passes. Something frightful and beastly and terrible has been turned into one of the most beautiful things in the world. How is

this possible? Is it a lie, or what? Did Titian know
that really human life was awful, that it was nothing
but a slaughterhouse? Did Max know, when he painted
witty cleverly composed scenes of torture? Maybe
they knew, thought Henry, but I certainly don't and I
don't want to. And he thought of Cato now with a
horrified pity which was a sort of disgust, and he
gazed into the far depths of the great picture and he
prayed for himself—May I never see what he sees,
never know what he knows, never be where he is, so
help me God!'' (p. 327)

Henry's epiphany does have a restorative impact on his
life. Following this experience, he is finally able to talk to his
mother, and he tells her how much she made him suffer as a
child (p. 332). But his revelation, accompanied by a simulta-
neous rejection of his vision, indicates his low level of spiritual awareness. The title of his work on Max Beckmann's art,
*Screaming or Yawning,* shows two possible reactions for those
confronted by real pain and suffering: True to his spirituality,
Henry plans passive ignorance. He turns to the consolation of
Colette and decides to marry her; he will keep Laxlinden and
become a man of property. With these decisions, he also recognizes that he has lost his chance for any spiritual life: ''[As
a spiritual being] I'm done for. . . . Now I shall never live
simply and bereft as I ought to live. I have chosen a mediocre
destiny. . . . I have failed, but I don't care. I shall be happy''
(p. 360).

### The Servants (1981)

A three-act opera by William Mathias, with libretto by Iris Murdoch, *The Servants* is based on the play *The Servants and the Snow* (discussed earlier in this chapter).[29] The themes remain the same, but Murdoch cut the play by half for the libretto.[30] Two of the original characters are cut (Grundig the bailiff and Frederic, Basil's valet), and a chorus of servants is added to reveal the servants' pain and fear giving the opera parallels to Greek tragedy. Murdoch also mentions that, in rewriting the play, "William Mathias insisted on building up the character of Marina into "a kind of priestess."[31] *The Servants* was first performed by Welsh National Opera at Cardiff New Theatre on September 15, 1980.

### The Black Prince (play) (1989)

Iris Murdoch's narrative style, in which interior monologues reveal motivation for action and complex plotting involves a large cast of characters, makes it difficult to present the full texture of the novels in the pared-down drama form. This is particularly true of the adaptation of the novel *The Black Prince* into a two-act play. However, the Hamlet-like soliloquies of the protagonist, Bradley Pearson (himself a Hamlet-like character), did work well for staging individual scenes. The play was first performed on April 25, 1989, at the Aldwych Theatre, London, where the cast was cut to a bare six main characters (Bradley Pearson, his ex-wife, his sister,

## OTHER NOVELS AND PLAYS

and the three members of the Baffin family) and three policemen.[32] It was well-cast, with Ian McDiarmid playing the lead, and well-received by the public but did not enjoy a long run.

## *Notes*

1. Iris Murdoch, *The Sandcastle* (New York: Viking Press, 1957), p. 232; subsequent references to this work are noted parenthetically in the text.

2. See Jack Turner, "Murdoch vs. Freud in *A Severed Head* and Other Novels," *Literature and Psychology* 36, nos. 1–2 (1990): 110–21.

3. Iris Murdoch, *A Severed Head* (New York: Viking Press, 1961), p. 14; subsequent references to this work are noted parenthetically in the text.

4. John Fletcher, "A Novelist's Plays: Iris Murdoch and the Theatre," *Essays in Theatre* 4, no. 1 (1985): 4.

5. Fletcher, p. 4.

6. Iris Murdoch and J. B. Priestley, *A Severed Head: A Play in Three Acts* (London: Chatto & Windus, 1964), p. 7.

7. See John Fletcher and Cheryl Bove, *A Primary and Secondary Bibliography, 1933–1989* (New York: Garland, 1993).

8. Fletcher, "A Novelist's Plays," p. 4.

9. Ibid., p. 6.

10. Ibid., pp. 13 and 15.

11. Iris Murdoch, *The Red and the Green* (New York: Viking Press, 1965), p. 298; subsequent references to this work are noted parenthetically in the text.

12. Lorna Sage and Malcolm Bradbury, "Iris Murdoch Talks to Lorna Sage and Malcolm Bradbury," *University of East Anglia Interviews,* taped on October 20, 1976 (AVC 1043).

13. Fletcher, "A Novelist's Plays," p. 7.

14. Iris Murdoch, *The Three Arrows and The Servants and the Snow* (New York: Viking Press, 1973), p. 39; subsequent references to this work are noted parenthetically in the text.

15. Peter Conradi, *Iris Murdoch: The Saint and the Artist* (New York: St. Martin's Press, 1986), p. 66.

16. Iris Murdoch, *An Accidental Man* (New York: Viking Press, 1971), p. 424; subsequent references to this work are noted parenthetically in the text.

17. A. S. Byatt, "Now Read On," interview broadcast by BBC Radio 4 on October 27, 1971. Tape M4256R, National Sound Archives, London.

18. Other characters prominently associated with Peter Pan include Randall Peronett (*An Unofficial Rose*), Hilary Burde (*A Word Child*), and Edward Baltram (*The Good Apprentice*).

19. *The Three Arrows and The Servants and the Snow* (New York: Viking Press, 1973). According to the stage directions to Act I, scene iv (p. 155), the monks all speak with Irish accents. The dialect "You chaps got anything to drink?" appears in Act I, scene i (p. 122).

20. Hugh Hebert, "The Iris Problem," *The Guardian* (October 24, 1972): 10.

21. "Lorna Sage has shown the echo of Titian's *Sacred and Profane Love* both in Rosa and Mischa's last tableau in *The Flight from the Enchanter* as well as in *The Sacred and Profane Love Machine*" (Conradi, p. 75).

22. For other treatments of the ménage à trois in Murdoch's novels, see *The Message to the Planet* and *The Sacred and Profane Love Machine*.

23. Iris Murdoch, *The Sacred and Profane Love Machine* (New York: Viking Press, 1974), p. 269; subsequent references to this work are noted parenthetically in the text.

24. Conradi, p. 210.

25. Iris Murdoch, *A Word Child* (New York: Viking Press, 1975), p. 18; subsequent references to this work are noted parenthetically in the text.

26. The Peter Pan motif figures significantly in *The Good Apprentice, An Unofficial Rose, The Philosopher's Pupil, An Accidental Man,* and *Henry and Cato* and to a lesser extent in *The Unicorn*.

27. Iris Murdoch, *Henry and Cato* (New York: Viking Press, 1976), p. 4; subsequent references to this work are noted parenthetically in the text.

28. Iris Murdoch accepted a fellowship at Washington University, St. Louis, Missouri, in the 1970s. While there, she was able to view several paintings by Max Beckmann, a German expressionist whose works were blacklisted as decadent by the Nazis. Following the Second World War, Beckmann accepted a teaching position at Washington University. Suffering and anguish are the topics of many of his paintings.

# OTHER NOVELS AND PLAYS

29. *The Servants: Opera in Three Acts,* Music by William Mathias, libretto by Iris Murdoch, (London: Oxford University Press, 1981).

30. Ruth Pitchford, "Iris Murdoch set to music," *Western Mail* (September 12, 1980).

31. Tom Sutcliffe, *The Guardian* (September 15, 1980): 9.

32. Iris Murdoch, *Three Plays: The Servants and the Snow; The Three Arrows; The Black Prince* (London: Chatto & Windus, 1989), pp. 303, 321.

# CHAPTER EIGHT

# The Gothic

At two separate symposiums on her novels at the Université de Caen (France), Iris Murdoch made known her objections to being classified as a Gothic novelist. While she defended herself against the term, she admitted that *The Unicorn* does have the trappings of a Gothic novel: "I'm not a gothic novelist. This happens to be 'a gothic novel' in that it's got the form of the arrival at the mysterious castle and the monster and the captivity and the mystery and so on, and that just belongs to this novel."[1] Earlier, at a 1978 symposium, she had remarked on the limited perception of such a term: "I don't like it as a general word about the novels because . . . it gives you a certain way of looking at the stuff which I think is rather limiting. . . . I would not like to be labelled as a Gothic novelist. I would regard this as limiting in a slightly derogatory sense."[2]

Although Murdoch eschews the term, many critics in America, England, and France have described several of her novels as Gothic. At least five strongly emphasize Gothic motifs and can be considered Gothic novels. Some of these, par-

## THE GOTHIC

ticularly *The Flight from the Enchanter, Bruno's Dream,* and *The Unicorn,* have received other critical acclaim, yet this genre is generally not considered Murdoch's strongest work.

### *The Flight from the Enchanter* (1956)

*The Flight from the Enchanter,* Murdoch's second published novel, introduces in her work the concept of the power figure, the enchanter, who reappears frequently in later novels. In *The Flight from the Enchanter* Mischa Fox and his alter ego, Calvin Blick, are the dark figures. This novel also emphasizes the instability and fear in the lives of immigrants, a topic arising from Murdoch's postwar work with refugees through the United Nations Relief and Rehabilitation Association. In the book, the two Lusiewicz brothers and Nina the dressmaker are victims; the Lusiewicz brothers turn to power to establish some control over their lives, but Nina's fear causes her to commit suicide.[3]

The novel also entertains an amusing, some may feel too light-hearted, look at the suffragette movement through events surrounding the financial difficulties of *The Artemis,* a women's review. *The Artemis,* founded by suffragettes, is now edited by a man, Hunter Keepe, whose mother was one of its founders. A gathering of the remaining original shareholders provides the reader with a glimpse of some singularly eccentric elderly women; one founding member, Camilla Wingfield, saves the review and ensures that it will have a female editor in the future.

The controlling women's theme is continued into the work place through John Rainborough, a civil servant who is head of the finance department with the Special European Labour Immigration Board (SELIB). Although the bureaucracy of SELIB could be said to rival that described in Charles Dicken's Circumlocution Department, SELIB seems to have been taken over by the female assistants to the male department heads. Rainborough even finds himself engaged to his own personal assistant, Agnes Casement, and requires the help of another woman friend, Marcia Cockeyne, in breaking the engagement.

But the man who wants to buy *The Artemis,* Mischa Fox, illustrates the main themes of the novel, the destructiveness of power and the necessity for responsibility. Iris Murdoch has noted that "characters who want to be manipulated by others" interest her and appear frequently in her novels: "People very often elect a god in their lives, they elect somebody whose puppet they want to be, and . . . almost subconsciously, are ready to receive suggestions from this person."[4] Such behavior becomes a way of avoiding truth, of living safely and without responsibility. Forcing others to take up positions of power removes responsibility for actions and continues the illusions which one finds comfortable.

An enigmatic enchanter whose mysterious background enhances his attractiveness to others, the aptly named Mischa Fox is the power figure of this novel. He possesses the physical and spiritual characteristics of the Gothic protagonist: besides being powerful, he is dark, harsh, and often described in predatory terms. Mischa has a sallow, hawk-like face,[5] the face of a demon (p. 219), and exceptional eyes which appear "wide and serene" (p. 205) and recall those of Melmoth (in Charles Maturin's *Melmoth the Wanderer*). Other features which indicate his Gothic association are his age, background, and identification with animals. According to John Rainborough, Mischa's age and origin are mysterious: "No one knows Mischa's age. One can hardly even make a guess. It's uncanny. He could be thirty, he could be fifty-five. . . . No one knows where he came from either. Where was he born? What blood is in his veins? No one knows" (p. 38). The blood reference here has both alien and vampire associations. Later references to the "extra ordinary flexibility of his feet and ankles," which are described as similar to the "smoothly bending limbs of an animal" (p. 205), suggest something satanic.

Like most Gothic protagonists, Mischa Fox appears most comfortable in darkness and in subterranean dwellings. When Rosa Keepe visits Mischa's Italian villa, she arrives to find him installed in a dark room (pp. 296–97). But the bizarre structure of Mischa's London house would rival houses in the best Gothic novels:

Mischa [bought] four houses in Kensington, two adjoining in one road, and two adjoining in the next road, and standing back to back with the first two. He had joined this block of four houses into one by building a square structure to span the gap. Within this strange *palazzo* . . . the walls and ceilings and stairs have been so much altered, improved and removed that very little remained of the original interiors. (p. 200)

Mischa's relationships with the characters in this novel involve both fear and attraction. Some believe he has knowledge of oriental magic (p. 151), and Rosa Keepe believes he knows all (p. 307). John Rainborough also has mixed feelings about Mischa: "[He] would have said sincerely . . . that Mischa Fox was one of his best friends; yet in his heart he now felt fear and almost hatred of the man" (pp. 31–32). Rainborough recognizes Mischa as a man "capable of enormous cruelty" (p. 33), and Mrs. Wingfield calls him "a bit of a press Lord and general mischief maker" (p. 126).

Those whose lives have been touched by Mischa also feel he is directing their fate. Even Calvin Blick, Mischa's malevolent and strong-armed associate, who uses blackmail to enforce Mischa's will, feels completely under his employer's control. Because Blick is described as "the dark half of Mischa's mind" (p. 35), some critics view the two as spiritual halves of the same person.[6] When Rosa contemptuously tells Blick that she can't understand why Mischa did not kill him years ago, Blick replies softly: "Mischa did kill me years ago" (p. 306). Thus Calvin Blick, like Peter Crean-Smith's Gerald Scottow in *The Unicorn*, performs his master's bidding after having been broken by him. These characters continue the cycle of power and suffering inherent in the concept of Até, which is addressed in *The Unicorn;* those who do not love sufficiently will pass their suffering on to others.

Mischa Fox's primary occupation appears to be controlling those who surround him, and his plotting and manipulation of others illustrate the interconnectedness of all things. For example, Rosa Keepe is terrorized by the two Polish im-

migrants Jan and Stefan Lusiewicz. The Lusiewicz brothers
are in England training under the SELIB scheme. Originally
victims of power, they turn to power themselves to establish
dominance over Rosa, who has befriended them and is teaching them English. Terrified into a sexual relationship with
both brothers, Rosa finally decides that "only darkness could
cast out darkness" (p. 256), and she appeals to Mischa Fox for
help. By doing so, she realizes that she has placed herself under Mischa's power (p. 263), but she is ignorant of the far-
reaching tentacles of her request. When Mischa causes a
question to be raised in the House of Commons concerning the
status of immigrants born west of the arbitrarily established
FPE (Farthest Point East), the Lusiewicz brothers (who are
working in England illegally) disappear from Rosa's life. But
an innocent immigrant, Nina the dressmaker, commits suicide
when she realizes that she was born on the wrong side of the
FPE; her fear and alienation are such that she does not understand that there will be no further follow-up to the question
brought up in the House.

### The Unicorn (1963)

The Unicorn has incident, theme, and setting characteristic of the Gothic novel. The Irish landscape in which it is
situated includes ancient dolmens and megaliths. Great cliffs
of black sandstone overlook a dark coastline and a cold, killing sea; and bogs, caves, and underground rivers give relief
to the generally barren inland. Gaze, an eighteenth-century

castle surrounded by wrecked gardens, sequesters a beautiful lady whose cortege includes a courtly lover and a page. The novel abounds in legends and in magical signs and occasions. Some of the local inhabitants are said to be related to fairies.

Married to her cousin Peter, Hannah Crean-Smith is sequestered at Gaze Castle for having pushed him over a sea cliff during an argument about her affair with Pip Lejour. Peter survived the fall, but departed for New York, leaving one of his lovers, Gerald Scottow, in charge of Hannah's imprisonment at Gaze. A local man, Denis Nolan, acts as her page,[7] and Effingham Cooper, a conventional civil servant from London, plays the part of the quester, visiting the Lejours at their nearby estate, Riders, and loving Hannah from afar. Another outsider, Marian Taylor, comes to Gaze castle to tutor Hannah in French. The principal plot addresses the outsiders' attempt to rescue Hannah; their rescue is botched, but it appears unlikely that Hannah wants to be rescued.

According to Iris Murdoch, the Cluny tapestries brought about the idea of *The Unicorn*.[8] The motifs on these medieval tapestries include a woman and a unicorn, which signifies purity and suffering. The main themes of the novel are "captivity and penance and power."[9] Hannah Crean-Smith is the obvious captive victim, but other characters too are held at Gaze through love and hate, which may also become forms of power. In this novel, Murdoch develops the Greek concept of Até in conjunction with penance as a sign of moral awareness.

Although it initially appears that Hannah is the unicorn of the title, a better reading would show Denis Nolan to be.[10] A curious mix of Gothic and spiritual, Denis is a local man believed to possess fairy blood. He is chaste and fey (p. 230), loves Hannah selflessly, and is seen as a Christ figure (p. 229). He willingly accepts the suffering of the Gaze household and, in accordance with Até, expiates the guilt of the household because he is able to accept suffering without passing it on to others.

Denis's functions as truth-teller and healer of the kingdom are denoted by his eyes, which are emblematic of knowledge and clear vision. They are variously described as "very blue," "striking," and "fierce" (pp. 39, 41, 172). And when Marian associates his glance with "the flash of a kingfisher" (p. 41), there are also connotations of the ritual fisher king.[11] Denis first appears in the novel carrying a tin bowl containing a large sick goldfish (Strawberry Nose), which he nurses back to health. And throughout the story he tends the salmon pool, netting it to keep the cranes (perhaps representing the Crean-Smiths) from eating the fish. Later, when Denis leaves Gaze, he catches Strawberry Nose to take away with him (p. 299). This extensive association with fish indicates that Denis is a life force and also blends with his task of healing the kingdom. Ritualistically, the fisher king must be healed by the questing knight before health and prosperity can return to the kingdom, but in this situation Denis himself heals the kingdom by vicariously expiating the guilt of the household.

Denis also develops many of Iris Murdoch's ideas about suffering. For Murdoch, suffering is a natural condition for humans because of their unenlightened condition, and, because of their spiritual depravity, their suffering is imperfect and ineffective. Denis hates Peter for his cruel treatment of

Hannah. His imperfect suffering has failed to expiate his guilt for this hatred, and Denis murders Peter by driving their car into the sea when Peter returns to Gaze. Had he turned only to love, Denis believes he might have saved Hannah who committed suicide rather than face Peter's return: "But I did not only love, I also hated. And hatred can corrupt the love that makes it be" (p. 301).

The imperfect suffering which Murdoch calls natural for humans also becomes a source of power by which the sufferer draws others to his or her position. This situation is true for Hannah, who, although she seems to be weak, manipulates the other characters through her apparent suffering. In *The Unicorn,* one of the characters elaborates on this use of power, associated with a low level of spiritual maturity, in an explanation of Até:

> Até is the name of the almost automatic transfer of
> suffering from one being to another. Power is a form
> of Até. The victims of power, and any power has its
> victims, are themselves infected. They have to pass it
> on, to use power on others. . . . For the powerless, to
> be a complete victim, may be another source of power.
> But Good is non-powerful. And it is in the good that
> Até is finally quenched, and when it encounters a pure
> being who only suffers and does not attempt to pass
> the suffering on. (p. 107)

While most readers initially believe Hannah, who has been sequestered for seven years, to be the "pure being" who suffers, Hannah reveals her suffering to have been an illusion:

# THE GOTHIC

"It was your belief in the significance of my suffering that kept me going. Ah, how much I needed you all! I have battened upon you like a secret vampire. . . . I lived by your belief in my suffering. But I had no real suffering" (p. 249). Denis, on the other hand, willingly accepts the role of the victim who perfects his suffering, relating it to the good and thereby making it an effective means for expiating guilt. By his willingness to accept the guilt of the entire household at the end of the novel, Denis turns toward the good. Although the responsibility for Peter's death and Denis's hatred for Peter cannot be denied, Denis begins atonement for his transgressions, as well as those of the household, with his decision to leave Gaze and take their suffering with him.

### The Italian Girl (1964)

Perhaps Iris Murdoch's least successful novel, *The Italian Girl* considers the topics of sibling rivalry, displaced persons, suffering, and the Oedipal complex. The novel beings with the middle-aged narrator, Edmund Narraway, returning home for his mother's funeral. Narraway arrives at night as a reluctant intruder to a dark and forbidding family home, and he immediately wants to flee: "My mother's existence here had been the reason for my not coming. Now her non-existence would provide an even stronger reason" for leaving undetected.[12] The selfish and domineering mother, Lydia, had jealously and alternately loved each of her sons, Otto and Edmund, and her grandchild, Flora, which caused insecurity and estrangement for them all. Edmund confesses his estrangement from his brother: "Though I was bound to Otto by steely bonds more awful than the bonds of love, we had, on our rare meetings, but little to say to each other" (p. 19).

Otto, a stonemason, his wife, Isabel, and their daughter, Flora, all live in the family home. Isabel feels constricted by their life: "We are all prisoners here. We are like people in an engraving" (p. 33). And she looks to Edmund as the only person who can heal the family. But Edmund believes himself unworthy of the role which Isabel wants him to play (p. 61) and feels "awkward, alien, excluded. There was nothing [he] could do for these people" (p. 85). And, in fact, he complicates their lives more, for when Flora asks him for money for an abortion, he grabs her in an ardent manner and frightens her away.

Two wild and strange outsiders, Elsa and David Levkin, are Russian Jews, immigrants through whom the themes of displaced persons and suffering are continued in this novel. Levkin, who has also asked Edmund Narraway to stay and help them (p. 76), explains that his sister is obsessed with her heritage: "There are the Jews that suffer and the Jews that succeed, the dark Jews and the light Jews. . . . She is all memory—she remembers so much, she remembers the memories that are not her own. . . . So she will suffer, so she will die young, I do fear it" (p. 80). Both Levkins disrupt the lives of the household. Elsa has an affair with Otto, loving him because he is a "monster and a ruin" (p. 79), and David impregnates both Isabel and Flora. Although David had planned to avoid his sister's obsession, he decides to return to Lenin-

## THE GOTHIC

grad, where he faces certain grief, after Elsa dies in a fire. He cannot forsake his heritage, and he must suffer in his own place (p. 185).

The title character, Maria Magistretti, is a mother figure and Edmund Narraway's old nurse. But because she was one of a succession of Italian girls employed by Lydia, Edmund doesn't even remember her real name. Maria has possibly had a lesbian relationship with Lydia, but she replaces Lydia in a positive way by teaching Edmund how to love others. She suggests that Edmund apologize to Flora and he is able to do so. He also reconciles with Otto when the brothers discuss their mother's domineering behavior and forgive her for her treatment of them. After he realizes his life is a muddle, Edmund exhibits what Murdoch calls "otherness" in his description of Maria (now called Maggie): "I certainly now, and with a fresh sharpness, saw Maggie as a separate and private and unpredictable being. I endowed her, as it were, with those human rights, the right of secrecy, the right of surprise" (p. 162). Once he recognizes Maggie as a person separate from himself, Edmund seems capable of loving her; she becomes the "one person in the world for whom [he] could be complete" (p. 211). However, Edmund's change is unconvincing for the reader, and he remains, ultimately, an uninteresting character.

In an Oedipal ending to the novel, Edmund forms a romantic attachment with the nurse of his youth. He is not under the illusion that such a love will be without its attendant suffering: "Whatever joy or sorrow might come to me from this would be real and my own, I would be living at my own level and suffering in my own place" (p. 211). Although he has been unable to heal the others, Edmund has reconciled with his brother and has found the vision to begin thinking of others. Before taking Maggie home to Italy, Edmund visits Isabel (who has left Otto) and tells her that he will help her if she and her baby ever need him.

### The Time of the Angels (1966)

The central question in *The Time of the Angels* is the place of morality in a world which no longer believes in God. Murdoch develops this theme through Gothic motifs, especially a wasteland setting and an unbelieving Anglican priest, Carel Fisher, and through his more conventional brother, Marcus, who intends to write a philosophical treatise on morality in a world without God.

The problems of displacement and past are again considered through two Russian immigrants, the rectory porter Eugene Peshkov and his son Leo. Eugene's wife had died of tuberculosis in a refugee camp when Leo was two, and Eugene reared Leo alone, trying to instill in his son his own sense of Russian pride. However, Leo wants only to forget his Russian heritage and become English. Eugene, who has never tried to make a place for himself in English society, makes friends only with exiles and misfits like himself;[13] he exists in his past, dwelling on the pre-Revolutionary dreamland of his childhood. The Peshkovs' conflicting views about the past cause continual friction between them, and in a final act of defiance Leo steals his father's Russian icon for money for a girlfriend's abortion. Although he does eventually retrieve the icon, Leo does so not out of respect for his father's feelings but as a quest to make himself worthy of Elizabeth Fisher. After he is disillusioned by Elizabeth, Leo embraces his heritage and enters an English university to study both French and Russian. His nationality appears to have been so thoroughly ingrained in his consciousness that he cannot escape from it.

The central figure of *The Time of the Angels,* Carel Fisher, resembles the larger-than-life, powerful Gothic protagonist. An atheistic Anglican priest, he is the fisher king gone wrong, the estranged "saver" of souls who rules from a virtual wasteland. His parish, St. Eustace Watergate, is located in an abandoned, war-torn area of London; the rector's lodging is the only building standing in the parish. The eighteenth-century church was badly damaged by a bomb during the war, and only its Wren tower remains intact. A description of the grounds about the rectory conveys a literal "wilderness" and "waste land" (pp. 67, 24): "There were no houses, only a completely flat surface of frozen mud, through which the roadway passed, with small humps here and there under stiff frozen tarpaulins. It seemed to be a huge building site, but an abandoned one" (p. 24). Father Fisher's parish personifies the "ruined vestiges of archaic religious institutions" which William Axton lists as characteristic of the Gothic scene.[14] The structure of the parish has been destroyed figuratively and literally.

The subterranean passages in the novel belong to the underground railway. The ever-present rumblings from the trains adversely affect everyone in the household by interrupting

## UNDERSTANDING IRIS MURDOCH

sleep, disturbing dreams, and lending an ominous atmosphere to the setting. Pattie, the housekeeper, has particular subconscious and conscious connections with these labyrinthine passages. She is illegitimate, and the only information she has concerning her father is that he is Jamaican and works as a conductor on the underground railway. Since the rumblings of the railway are noted throughout the novel, Pattie cannot help being constantly reminded of her missing father and her unwelcome birth. Carel Fisher is also closely associated with labyrinthine passages. Although his room is on the second floor of the rectory, other characters must approach him by means of tunnels. His brother Marcus is repeatedly refused admittance to the rectory; his first entry into the building is through the coalhole during an electrical outage.

Darkness, in fact, is omnipresent in the novel. Fisher prefers the shadows to daylight and spends much of the day lying on his bed. He keeps his drapes drawn and places a scarf over the lamp shade to dim the light. Throughout the novel the rectory is enveloped by a fog so dense that it is impossible to see outside, and the interior of the house is very dim.

Elizabeth Fisher is the secluded maiden in *The Time of the Angels*. Her isolation is such that she is confined to her room throughout the novel. Although Eugene and Leo Peshkov live in the rectory basement, they are unaware of her presence until Carel's daughter Muriel tells them she is there, and any knowledge about Elizabeth comes primarily from other characters' discussions about her. She is incapacitated by a mysterious malady, a back ailment which resists diagnosis and treatment. Although thought to be Carel's orphaned niece, Elizabeth is actually his daughter by his sister-in-law, Sheila,

# THE GOTHIC

whom he had seduced as revenge when her husband, Julian, eloped with Anthea Barlow, the woman all three Fisher brothers had desired.

In some ways Elizabeth resembles Hannah Crean-Smith (*The Unicorn*). Everyone assumes she is innocent, but she is not. Carel insists that Elizabeth be sheltered from the outside world and forces Muriel to promise that she will abide by his wishes. Muriel, however, believes that Elizabeth is "far too delicious to be endlessly wasted in the dark, unvisited cavern-like environment which . . . [her] father increasingly created round about himself" (p. 44), and she takes Leo upstairs to view Elizabeth from a peephole in the linen closet. From her hiding spot, Muriel discovers Carel and Elizabeth's incestuous relationship when she sees their forms reflected in a large French mirror (pp. 176–77).

Carel, much like Mischa Fox (*The Flight from the Enchanter*), represents those who adulterate power; by dominating those surrounding him and forcing compliance with his own will, he works against the intent of the good. But he also experiences demons of his own; he is tormented and finally destroyed by his inability to endure his loss of faith. Thus through Carel Fisher Murdoch raises a fundamental question concerning her moral philosophy—what does morality entail in a world without belief in God?

Two of the Fisher brothers consider this subject at length in a dialect in which Marcus, in writing "a philosophical treatise upon morality in a secular age" (p. 19), acts as a foil for his eccentric brother's beliefs. Marcus, the spokesman for rationality, claims modern agnostic views, but he is actually quite conventional. Only Carel has truly considered the unthinkable. According to him, no one has really believed this concept before: "Oh yes, people have often uttered the words, but no one believed them. Perhaps Nietzsche did for a little. Only his egoism of an artist soon obscured the truth. He could not hold it. Perhaps that was what drove him mad. Not the truth itself but his failure to hold it in contemplation" (p. 183). Carel tells his brother, "We are creatures of accident, operated by forces we do not understand" (p. 185). The title of the novel refers to the angels, the other spiritual powers, who take over the vacuum caused by the death of God: "The disappearance of God does not simply leave a void into which human reason can move. The death of God has set the angels free. And they are terrible" (p. 185). Really imagining the consequences of a world without God brings horror and despair to Carel. Because he lacks the virtue necessary for perfection, he cannot accept a spiritual world which offers only torment and no consolation, so he resorts to the only form of consolation available to him—use of power. His threadbare carpet and constant pacing are symbolic of his desire to escape his unsettled spirituality, and his use of power evidences his will to wrestle these manifestations into an order over which he has control. But when these efforts fail to release him from his torments, Carel Fisher finally escapes to an unknown world by suicide.

### *The Italian Girl* (play) (1968)

*The Italian Girl* was adapted for the stage by James Saunders and Iris Murdoch, and, although the play was published in an acting edition, a book edition, and a German edition,[15] the adaptation seems to have been unsuccessful.

Murdoch has commented that the collaboration was rushed and that the play turned out more comic than the novel had been.[16] During its production at the Wyndham Theatre, London, she talked to Ronald Bryden about her difficulty with the play form and gave some reasons why the adaptation was not successful: "To present something in the play form is alien to me, in that the kind of things I want to meditate on, as it were, demand continuous prose."[17] She also claims that staging *The Italian Girl* brought about its weaknesses:

> One sees which characters are really live ones and which are pretty cardboard: in *The Italian Girl,* I think there are three live ones and three which are difficult to animate on the stage. Also the structure of the book emerges very clearly. . . . There's a weak point about two-thirds of the way through which is less obvious in the novel but comes across very clearly, I'm afraid, on the stage.[18]

Although Murdoch does not identify the flaw to which she refers, most critics would agree that the amelioration of Edmund's character, which begins about two-thirds of the way into the play, is unconvincing. In addition, John Fletcher also points out that the characters are not attractive, and "the dénouement [is] too rushed to develop convincingly an argument . . . about Edmund's spiritual renewal and Otto's seeing himself truly."[19]

### *Bruno's Dream* (1969)

*Bruno's Dream* is well known for its vivid London descriptions, especially of Brompton cemetery and the Chelsea and Battersea areas. The "bunchy brown granite pillars" inside the Servite Church on Fulham Road, where Miles meditates, are typical of the realistic descriptions of Murdoch's London.[20]

Like that of *The Unicorn,* the setting in *Bruno's Dream* is oppressive, with Bruno's shabby Stadium Street house darkened by continual rain and an eventual flooding of the Thames. The novel concerns the spiritual awakening of the dying Bruno Greensleave and some of his family members. A failed artist, Bruno has a fascination with spiders; he had planned several books on them but has published only a few articles. Bruno and his son, Miles, a failed poet, have been estranged for the past ten years. Now that Bruno is dying, Miles visits him, but he seems primarily interested in Bruno's very valuable stamp collection. Miles's first wife, an Indian girl named Parvati, died in an airplane accident; he is now married to Diana, an unsuccessful commercial artist.

Bruno is attended to by Danby Odell, the widower of Bruno's daughter, Gwen, who had drowned in the Thames trying to save a child who had fallen from a barge (p. 25). Danby, a mild-mannered and carefree "shambler through pubs" (p. 5), is liked by "almost everybody" (p. 20). He has been a kind son-in-law for Bruno and runs the Greensleave printing works for him (p. 8). Nigel Boase and his cousin, Adelaide, a maid with whom Danby has had a casual affair, live with

Danby. Nigel acts as companion and nurse to Bruno. A quiet and gentle man, Nigel loves Danby and writes to him about the significance of love:

> "Love is a strange thing. . . . It is a weird thought that anyone is *permitted* to love anyone and in any way he pleases. Nothing in nature forbids it. A cat may look at a king, the worthless can love the good, the good the worthless, the worthless the worthless and the good the good. . . . Anything can happen, so that in a way, a terrible terrible way, there are no impossibilities." (pp. 285–86)

Nigel's philosophy apparently reflects Murdoch's beliefs, for her novels, including *Bruno's Dream*, abound with unlikely attractions.

The sequestered virgin in the story is Lisa Watkins, Miles's sister-in-law, who lives with Miles and her sister, Diana. Lisa had obtained a first in "Greats" (classical languages, literature and philosophy) at Oxford, taught school in Yorkshire, and joined the Communist Party (p. 66). She then converted to Catholicism, entered an order of nuns called the Poor Clares, and went to Paris to perform social work. There she contracted tuberculosis, and she later returned to England and left the convent. After a convalescence period spent with Diana and Miles, Lisa stayed on with them (p. 66), and they continued to treat her as an invalid: "Miles had come to think of her as a person secluded, segregated, enclosed" (p. 156).

But Lisa proves herself capable; she becomes another willing nurse-companion for Miles's estranged and elderly father when Miles and Diana cannot bring themselves to look after him. Miles has difficulty communicating with Bruno, and both Miles and Diana are so repulsed by his alarming appearance that they are unable to touch him. Lisa, however, takes Bruno's hand (p. 124) and calms his fears about death, just as she (and not Diana) had comforted her father before he died (p. 137).

With the exception of Nigel, all of the characters love selfishly. Danby takes his affair with Adelaide quite casually and even "cashiered Adelaide on the spot, provisionally of course" (p. 106) when he became attracted to Diana. Later he transfers his affections to Lisa. Bruno, too, has loved unwisely. Early in his marriage to Janie, who has been dead for forty years, Bruno had an affair with a woman named Maureen. Janie found out about it, and they had terrible quarrels over Maureen which they were unable to forget. Bruno has never forgiven himself for ignoring Janie's calls when she was dying; he did not go to her because he was afraid she might curse him instead of forgive him for his affair. Miles, too, has a warped perception of love. Although he is still obsessed with his first wife, Parvati, and unable to bring himself to forget her or forgive his father for not quite approving of their marriage, Miles secretly loves his sister-in-law, Lisa.

An ironic reversal illustrates that Lisa's spirituality, much like Hannah Crean-Smith's (*The Unicorn*), is a false perception on the part of others. Lisa had discovered on Miles and Diana's wedding day that she loved Miles, but she had kept her feelings to herself as a sort of sacrifice. Later her sequestered situation led Danby and Miles to fall in love with her, and each

## THE GOTHIC

man believed her to be held in reserve for himself. However, when Danby presses Lisa for attention, she agrees to rejoin the world for him:

> I want to get over Miles and I will get over Miles. . . . Miles feels I'm unattainable, as an angel. It will hurt terribly when it turns out that I am only a woman after all. . . . I am not mad, Danby. I have never been more sane, coldly sane, *self-interestedly* sane. . . . I want warmth and love, affection, laughter, happiness, all the things I'd done without. . . . You imagine I'm good. But those self-denying years prove nothing. (pp. 295–96)

With the recovery of her egoism, Lisa takes the first steps towards reestablishing her own life by telling Miles of her love and Danby of his false image of her. Had she merely gone away to India, she would have continued her image of self-sacrifice: "A Lisa in India would have become a divinity. A Lisa sitting in Danby's car with an arm outstretched along the back of the seat, as Diana had last seen her, was fallen indeed" (p. 308).

As Lisa and Danby fall to the hedonism of fast cars, expensive clothes, and fine restaurants, their responsibilities with Bruno are taken over by Diana. The two sisters actually exchange spiritual positions; Lisa looks younger and radiant, and Diana sits with Bruno, learning to console and love him. But Bruno has become more lovable. As he nears death, he discovers the importance of love and realizes how badly he has loved:

## UNDERSTANDING IRIS MURDOCH

One sees now how pointless it all was, all the things
one chased after, all the things one wanted. . . . He
had loved only a few people and loved them so badly,
so selfishly. He had made a muddle of everything.
Was it only in the presence of death that one could see
so clearly what love ought to be like? If only the
knowledge which he had now, this absolute nothing-
else-matters, could somehow go backwards and purify
the little selfish loves and straighten out the muddles.
(pp. 304–05)

## *Notes*

1. "Discussion sur *The Unicorn*," *Gaéliana* no. 5 (1983): 203. [Publi-
cation of conference papers and discussion on *The Unicorn* at the Centre de
Recherches de Littérature, de Civilisation et Linguistique des Pays de Langue
Anglaise, l'université de Caen (France)].

2. Jean-Louis Chevalier, ed., *Recontres avec Iris Murdoch* (Caen: Centre
de Recherches de Littérature et Linguistique des Pays de Langue Anglaise,
1978), p. 85.

3. In *Iris Murdoch: The Saint and the Artist* (New York: St. Martin's
Press, 1986), Peter Conradi notes that an early draft of the novel (in the Murdoch manuscripts at the University of Iowa) indicates that "all the major characters were to have been refugees. . . . The published book distances this
theme of displacement" (p. 52).

4. Chevalier, p. 76.

5. Iris Murdoch, *The Flight from the Enchanter* (New York: Viking
Press, 1956), p. 226; subsequent references to this work are noted parenthetically in the text.

6. Conradi, p. 53. Peter Conradi quotes Iris Murdoch as saying that
"Blick represents Fox's 'sub-conscious' dark half."

# THE GOTHIC

7. Iris Murdoch, *The Unicorn* (New York: Viking Press, 1963), p. 44; subsequent references to this work are noted parenthetically in the text.

8. Iris Murdoch describes how the tapestries related to her writing *The Unicorn:* "I think the germ for this book came a very long time before I wrote it, when I first saw the Cluny tapestries." (*Gaéliana,* p. 195).

9. *Gaéliana,* p. 195.

10. At the discussion of *The Unicorn* published in *Gaéliana,* Murdoch indicated that Denis Nolan was a forerunner of her good character from *A Fairly Honourable Defeat,* Tallis Browne.

11. Jessie L. Weston discusses the prevalence of the fisher king motif in quest literature in her book *From Ritual to Romance* (New York: Doubleday Anchor Books, 1957), pp. 114–36.

12. Iris Murdoch, *The Italian Girl* (New York: Viking Press, 1964), p. 5; subsequent references to this work are noted parenthetically in the text.

13. Iris Murdoch, *The Time of the Angels* (New York: Viking Press, 1966), p. 50; subsequent references to this work are noted parenthetically in the text.

14. William F. Axton, introduction to *Melmoth the Wanderer* by Charles Robert Maturin (Lincoln: University of Nebraska Press, 1961), p. viii.

15. See John Fletcher and Cheryl Bove, *Iris Murdoch: A Primary and Secondary Bibliography, 1933–1989* (New York: Garland, 1993).

16. W. K. Rose, "Iris Murdoch, Informally," *London Magazine* 8 (June 1968): 59–60.

17. Ronald Bryden, "Talking to Iris Murdoch," *The Listener* 79 (April 4, 1968): 433.

18. Ibid., p. 433.

19. John Fletcher, "A Novelist's Plays: Iris Murdoch and the Theatre," *Essays in Theatre* 4, no. 1 (1985): 6.

20. Iris Murdoch, *Bruno's Dream* (New York: Viking Press, 1969), p. 184; subsequent references to this work are noted parenthetically in the text. For further information on Murdoch's London settings see Louis L. Martz, "Iris Murdoch: The London Novels," in *Twentieth Century Literature in Retrospect,* ed. Reuben A. Brower (Cambridge, Harvard University Press, 1971), pp. 65–86.

# CHAPTER NINE

# Conclusion

Although Iris Murdoch has consistently claimed that she is not a philosophical novelist, it is impossible to read her works without considering her moral philosophy, for her aesthetics and moral philosophy are inextricable. Through her understanding of the human psyche and the motivations for human behavior Murdoch presents characters who are the progeny of both Plato and Freud. Individuals live in a world of illusion and possess a low level of awareness because they must necessarily be concerned with themselves. Their fundamental concerns are solipsistic because the ego acts as the psyche's protective device, and human instincts are for self-preservation.

Murdoch's moral philosophy discounts the existence of a traditional God, and she does not believe in an afterlife; however, she would like to maintain the structure of religion by replacing God with good. She would propose that individuals be good for nothing, without any ulterior motivation such as reward or punishment in an afterlife. This idea has remained fairly constant in her essays and novels through the years; however, her concept of God has recently evolved in that she

## CONCLUSION

appears more interested in developing eccentric religious figures who accept a universal form of various doctrines. She apparently had no difficulty discarding the idea of a traditional God in the Marxism of her youth, but now Murdoch has adopted a combination of Jewish, Christian, and Buddhist ideals. Her recent works favor Anglican priests who have lost their faith, do not hold traditional doctrine, and are open to alternative views of religion.[1]

Unlike moral philosophers who only discuss ethics, Murdoch would propose a means of perfection. She believes that to move to a higher level of awareness, toward good and truth, individuals must sublimate their egos and attend to others. Attention removes one's focus from oneself and allows a consideration of others which opens one to a more truthful view of the world. Murdoch suggests in *The Sovereignty of Good* that individuals can improve morally by focusing their attention on valuable things such as virtuous people, great art, and the idea of goodness itself (p. 56).

The idea of art as a means of changing consciousness is shown throughout her writings. Any art, including such expressions as painting, music, dance, theater, and literature, can illuminate if it is great enough. Literature, for example, conveys fundamental truths across cultures and through generations. Murdoch says in the essay "Existentialists and Mystics" that "we today have no great or essential difficulty in understanding plays written by Greeks in the fifth century B.C. We make, in many respects though not in all, the same kinds of moral judgements as the Greeks did, and we recognize good or decent people in times and literatures remote from our own.''[2] As an example, she notes that it is just as important for Patroclus to be kind to the captive women in the *Iliad* as it is that Emma should be kind to Miss Bates in Jane Austen's *Emma* (p. 177); and she calls this recognizable truth ''testimony to the existence of a single durable human nature'' (p. 178).

Because of the truth-conveying properties of art, Murdoch believes artists have a messianic duty to present reality in their art. Thus her aesthetics emphasize the importance of realism in the novel, and she regrets the experimental nature of the modern novel and its lack of adequate and truthful characterization. She identifies with the nineteenth-century realist tradition and would like to portray characters who are real and various and representative of life. One of her gifts in characterization is her patient and loving presentation of her characters. The reader never feels, as might be the case with an author such as D. H. Lawrence, that Murdoch has distaste or condescension for any of her characters, even her most self-centered people or evil power figures. She is, as it were, applying the just and loving gaze to her characters which she would encourage from her reader.

As she explains in the essay ''Against Dryness: A Polemical Sketch,'' modern philosophical views of man fail to present a convincing account of the inner life, which Murdoch believes is necessary for changing consciousness and moving one toward awareness.[3] Consequently, she feels that modern literature is inaccurate as an art form. For example, modern literature is often concerned with violence, but it has few convincing pictures of evil (p. 20). She thinks that the artist should use imagination, not fantasy, to portray the rich texture of actual experience. Literature can promote moral awareness by showing people the truth about themselves.

Although the artist has an obligation to portray truth in art, this does not necessarily mean that the work must be somber and serious. In fact, Murdoch believes the novel should be a comic form because an accurate description of life would be funny:

> I think all novels are comic forms—yes, *all* novels. If one's going to portray human life in the way that a novel does, or at least the traditional novel does, you can't avoid being funny, because human life *is* funny. Any prolonged description of anything produces something funny. Somehow any prolonged texture of a story has places for wit and places where the thing is absurd.[4]

Consequently, her vision, which reveals the lengths to which humans are willing to go to protect their images of themselves, is funny.

For Murdoch, the artist who truly apprehends the existence of others has virtue,[5] and she would encourage the writer to attend carefully in order to reveal the greatest amount of truth possible. In "The Sublime and Beautiful Revisited" she states, "The great novelist is essentially tolerant, that is, displays a real apprehension of persons other than the author as having a right to exist and to have a separate mode of being

# UNDERSTANDING IRIS MURDOCH

which is important and interesting'' (p. 257). The task which she sets in ''Against Dryness'' for the modern novelist is ''to write the best book he knows how to write'' (p. 16), and part of the task is to continue to bring out the next novel to correct the mistakes of the last'' (p. 15). Human imperfection precludes successful completion of the artists's task. But this failure should also become a starting point: ''To speak of failure here has nothing disgraceful about it. Almost every work of art is a failure. The point is that this particular type of failure is one that we ought never to cease worrying about'' (''The Sublime and Beautiful Revisited,'' p. 266).

When Linda Wertheimer asked Iris Murdoch about the message in the title of her latest work, *The Message to the Planet,* Murdoch replied: ''The message is—everything is contingent. There are no deep foundations. Our life rests on chaos and rubble, and all we can try to do is be good.''[6] Murdoch's message has not changed considerably throughout forty years of writing. It has become more complex and highly textured by allusions, iconography, and comic irony, but the moral philosopher emerges from behind her realistic portrayal of unique individuals. And the Platonist in her concludes that individuals live in a world of illusion and will never know much. However, Murdoch maintains an optimism for the human race which belies her portrait of egoistic individuals who attend only to themselves and cling to the consolations of the world. The vision of truth is there, even if individuals can gain only intimations of it, and the artist who attends carefully in order to present a just and accurate vision will be an instrument of truth for the world.

## CONCLUSION

*Notes*

1. See Father McAlister (*The Book and the Brotherhood*) and Father Jacoby (*The Philosopher's Pupil*).

2. Iris Murdoch, "Existentialists and Mystics: A Note on the Novel in the New Utilitarian Age," in *Essays and Poems Presented to Lord David Cecil,* ed. W. W. Robson (London: Constable, 1970), p. 177; subsequent references to this essay are noted parenthetically in the text.

3. Iris Murdoch, "Against Dryness: A Polemical Sketch," *Encounter* 16, no. 1 (1961): 19; subsequent references to this essay are noted parenthetically in the text.

4. Stephanie Nettell, "Iris Murdoch: An Exclusive Interview," *Books and Bookmen* 8 (September 1966): 13.

5. Iris Murdoch, "The Sublime and Beautiful Revisited," *Yale Review* 49 (1959): 269; subsequent references to this essay are noted parenthetically in the text.

6. Linda Wertheimer, *All Things Considered,* National Public Radio (New York City studios), broadcast February 26, 1990.

# BIBLIOGRAPHY

## Works by Iris Murdoch

### Fiction

*Under the Net*. London: Chatto & Windus, 1954; New York: Viking Press, 1954.

*The Flight from the Enchanter*. London: Chatto & Windus, 1956; New York: Viking Press, 1956.

*The Sandcastle*. London: Chatto & Windus, 1957; New York: Viking Press, 1957.

*The Bell*. London: Chatto & Windus, 1958; New York: Viking Press, 1958.

*A Severed Head*. London: Chatto & Windus, 1961; New York: Viking Press, 1961.

*An Unofficial Rose*. London: Chatto & Windus, 1962; New York: Viking Press, 1962.

*The Unicorn*. London: Chatto & Windus, 1963; New York: Viking Press, 1963.

*The Italian Girl*. London: Chatto & Windus, 1964; New York: Viking Press, 1964.

*The Red and the Green*. London: Chatto & Windus, 1965; New York: Viking Press, 1965.

*The Time of the Angels*. London: Chatto & Windus, 1966; New York: Viking Press, 1966.

*The Nice and the Good*. London: Chatto & Windus, 1968; New York: Viking Press, 1968.

*Bruno's Dream*. London: Chatto & Windus, 1969; New York: Viking Press, 1969.

*A Fairly Honourable Defeat*. London: Chatto & Windus, 1970; New York: Viking Press, 1970.

*An Accidental Man*. London: Chatto & Windus, 1971; New York: Viking Press, 1972.

*The Black Prince*. London: Chatto & Windus, 1973; New York: Viking Press, 1973.

## 198

## BIBLIOGRAPHY

*The Sacred and Profane Love Machine*. London: Chatto & Windus, 1974; New York: Viking Press, 1974.

*A Word Child*. London: Chatto & Windus, 1975; New York: Viking Press, 1975.

*Henry and Cato*. London: Chatto & Windus, 1976; New York: Viking Press, 1977.

*The Sea, The Sea*. London: Chatto & Windus, 1978; New York: Viking Press, 1978.

*Nuns and Soldiers*. London: Chatto & Windus, 1980; New York: Viking Press, 1981.

*The Philosopher's Pupil*. London: Chatto & Windus, 1983; New York: Viking Press, 1983.

*The Good Apprentice*. London: Chatto & Windus, 1985; New York: Viking Press, 1986.

*The Book and the Brotherhood*. London: Chatto & Windus, 1987; New York: Viking Press, 1988.

*The Message to the Planet*. London: Chatto & Windus, 1989; New York: Viking Press, 1990.

**Plays**

Iris Murdoch and J. B. Priestley. *A Severed Head*. London: Chatto & Windus, 1964.

James Saunders and Iris Murdoch. *The Italian Girl*. London & New York: Samuel French, 1969.

*The Three Arrows* and *The Servants and the Snow*. London: Chatto & Windus, 1973; New York: Viking Press, 1974.

*Three Plays: The Servants and the Snow, The Three Arrows, The Black Prince*. London: Chatto & Windus, 1989.

*The Servants: An Opera in Three Acts* (Music by William Mathias, Libretto by Iris Murdoch). London: Oxford University Press, 1980.

**Philosophy**

*Sartre, Romantic Rationalist*. Cambridge: Bowes & Bowes, 1953; New Haven: Yale University Press, 1953.

# BIBLIOGRAPHY

*The Sovereignty of Good over Other Concepts.* London: Cambridge University Press, 1967; New York: Schocken Books, 1971.

*The Fire and the Sun: Why Plato Banished the Artists.* Oxford: Clarendon Press, 1977.

*Acastos: Two Platonic Dialogues.* London: Chatto & Windus, 1986.

**Poetry**

*A Year of Birds* (engravings by Reynolds Stone). Tisbury, England: Compton Press, 1978; London: Chatto & Windus, 1984.

"Too Late." *Boston University Journal* 23, no. 2 (1975): 29–31.

"John Sees a Stork at Zamorra." *Boston University Journal* 23, no. 2 (1975): 31.

"Agamemnon Class 1939." *Boston University Journal* 25, no. 2 (1977): 57–58.

"Poem and Egg." *Transatlantic Review* 60 (June 1977): 32–33.

"The Brown Horse." *Transatlantic Review* 60 (June 1977): 32–33.

"The Public Garden in Calimera." *Transatlantic Review* 60 (June 1977): 33–34.

"Motorist and Dead Bird." *The Listener* 97, no. 2513 (June 16, 1977): 781.

"Fox." *Poetry London/Apple Magazine*, edited by Tambimuttu, 1, no. 1 (Autumn 1979): 40.

"No Smell." *Poetry London/Apple Magazine*, edited by Tambimuttu, 1, no. 1 (Autumn 1979): 41.

"Gunnera." *Poetry London/Apple Magazine*, edited by Tambimuttu, 1, no. 1 (Autumn 1979): 41.

"Edible Fungi." *Poetry London/Apple Magazine*, edited by Tambimuttu, 1, no. 1 (Autumn 1979): 41–42.

"Music in Ireland." In *Occasional Poets*, ed. by Richard Adams. London: Viking, 1986. Pp. 126–28.

**Short Story**

"Something Special." *Winter's Tales* 3. Editor anon. London: Macmillan; New York: St. Martin's Press, 1957. Pp. 175–204.

# BIBLIOGRAPHY

**Selected Critical Essays**

"The Existentialist Hero." *The Listener* 43, no. 1104 (March 23, 1950): 523–24.

"Symposium: Thinking and Language." *Proceedings of the Aristotelian Society* Supplement 25 (1951): 25–34.

"Nostalgia for the Particular." *Proceedings of the Aristotelian Society* 52 (1952): 243–60.

"The Existentialist Political Myth." *Socratic Digest* (Oxford) 5 (1952): 52–63.

"Vision and Choice in Morality." *Aristotelian Society: Dreams and Self-Knowledge* Supplement 30 (1956): 32–58.

"T. S. Eliot as a Moralist." In *T. S. Eliot: A Symposium for his Seventieth Birthday,* edited by Neville Braybrooke. London: Rupert Hart-Davis; New York: Farrar, Straus, and Cudahay, 1958. Pp. 152–60.

"A House of Theory." In *Conviction,* ed. Norman Mackenzie. London: MacGibbon & Kee, 1958. Pp. 218–33.

"The Sublime and the Good." *Chicago Review* 13, no. 3 (Autumn 1959): 42–55.

"The Sublime and the Beautiful Revisited." *Yale Review* 49 (December 1959): 247–71.

"Against Dryness." *Encounter* 16, no. 1 (January 1961): 16–20.

"Morality and the Bomb." In *Women Ask Why: An Intelligent Woman's Guide to Nuclear Disarmament.* London: Campaign for Nuclear Disarmament, n.d. [1962]. Pp. 1–6.

"Freedom and Knowledge." In *Freedom and the Will,* ed. D. F. Pears. London: Macmillan; New York: St. Martin's Press, 1963. Pp. 80–104.

"The Idea of Perfection." *Yale Review* 53, no. 3 (Spring 1964): 342–80.

"The Moral Decision about Homosexuality." *Man and Society* 7 (Summer 1964): 3–6.

# BIBLIOGRAPHY

"The Darkness of Practical Reason." *Encounter* 27, no. 1 (July 1966): 46–50.

"Existentialists and Mystics: A Note on the Novel in the New Utilitarian Age." In *Essays and Poems Presented to Lord David Cecil,* ed. W. W. Robson. London: Constable, 1970. Pp. 169–83.

"Salvation by Words." *New York Review of Books* 18 (June 15, 1972): 3–5.

"Ethics and the Imagination." *Irish Theological Quarterly* 52, nos. 1–2 (1986): 81–95.

## Works about Iris Murdoch

### Selected Interviews

Atlas, James. "The Abbess of Oxford." *Vanity Fair* 51, no. 3 (March 1988): 70, 76, 80, 82, 86.

Barrows, John. "Living Writers—7: Iris Murdoch." *John O'London's* 4 (May 4, 1961): 498.

Bellamy, Michael O. "An Interview with Iris Murdoch." *Contemporary Literature* 18, no. 2 (Spring 1977): 129–40.

Biles, Jack I. "An Interview with Iris Murdoch." *Studies in the Literary Imagination* 12, no. 2 (1978): 115–25.

Blow, Simon. "An Interview with Iris Murdoch." *Spectator* 237 (September 15, 1976): 24–25.

Brans, Jo. "Virtuous Dogs and a Unicorn." In Bran's *Listen to the Voices: Conversations with Contemporary Writers.* Dallas: Southern Methodist University Press, 1988. Pp. 171–92.

Glover, Stephen. "Iris Murdoch Talks to Stephen Glover." *New Review* 3, no. 32 (November 1976): 56–59.

Hale, Sheila, and A. S. Byatt. "Women Writers Now: Their Approach and Apprenticeship." *Harpers and Queen* (October 1976): 178–91.

# BIBLIOGRAPHY

Heusel, Barbara Stevens. "An Interview with Iris Murdoch." *University of Windsor Review* (Windsor, Ontario) 21, no. 1 (Winter 1988): 1–13.

Heyd, Ruth. "An Interview with Iris Murdoch." *University of Windsor Review* (Windsor, Ontario) (Spring 1965): 138–43.

Kermode, Frank. "Myth, Reality and Fiction." *The Listener* 68, no. 1744 (August 30, 1962): 311–13.

Mehta, Ved. "Onward and Upward with the Arts: A Battle Against the Bewitchment of Our Intelligence." *New Yorker* 37 (December 9, 1961): 59–159. Iris Murdoch pp. 108, 110–112.

Meyers, Jeffrey. "The Art of Fiction CXVII: Iris Murdoch." *Paris Review* 115 (Summer 1990): 206–25.

Nettle, Stephanie. "Iris Murdoch: An Exclusive Interview." *Books and Bookmen* 11 (September 1966): 14–15, 66.

Rose, W. K. "Iris Murdoch, Informally." *Shenandoah* 19, no. 2 (1968): 3–22.

Slaymaker, William. "An Interview with Iris Murdoch." *Papers in Language and Literature* 21, no. 4 (Fall 1985): 425–32.

Ziegler, Heide, and Christopher Bigsby, eds. *The Radical Imagination and the Liberal Tradition: Interviews with English and American Novelists.* London: Junction Books, 1982. Pp. 209–30.

**Books**

Bloom, Harold, ed. *Iris Murdoch.* New York: Chelsea House Publishers, 1986. Part of the Modern Critical Views series; most of the thirteen critical essays in this collection concentrate on individual novels, though Shakespearean plot, London setting, and the Gothic novels are also considered; includes a bibliography.

Bove, Cheryl Browning. *A Character Index and Guide to the Fiction of Iris Murdoch.* New York: Garland Publishing, 1986. Introductory chapter on Murdoch's aesthetics and moral philosophy; annotated character and place name index for the novels from *Under the*

## BIBLIOGRAPHY

*Net* (1954) through *The Good Apprentice* (1985) and the dramas *The Servants and the Snow* and *The Three Arrows.*

Conradi, Peter J. *Iris Murdoch: The Saint and the Artist.* New York: St. Martin's Press, 1986. The most thorough and sensitive study of Murdoch's novels available; includes an excellent bibliography.

Dipple, Elizabeth. *Iris Murdoch: Work for the Spirit.* Chicago: University of Chicago Press, 1982. Addresses Murdoch's aesthetics and moral philosophy in connection with her characterization.

Hague, Angela. *Iris Murdoch's Comic Vision.* Cranbury, N.J.: Associated University Presses, 1984. Analyzes Murdoch as a comic novelist; proposes that her ironic tone and comic elements are as important to her fiction as her use of myth and philosophy.

Johnson, Deborah. *Iris Murdoch.* Bloomington: Indiana University Press, 1987. Study of Murdoch's novels based on feminist literary and psychoanalytic theory.

Mettler, Darlene D. *Sound and Sense: Musical Allusion and Imagery in the Novels of Iris Murdoch.* New York: Peter Lang, 1991. Examines the use of musical allusion and imagery, primarily in eight Murdoch novels.

Todd, Richard. *Iris Murdoch: The Shakespearian Interest.* New York: Barnes & Noble, 1979. Murdoch's interest in Shakespeare is shown in her novels, particularly in the revelation of self, the pairing of couples, and the use of characters who act as enchanters.

——— . *Iris Murdoch.* London and New York: Methuen, 1984. A critical study of Murdoch's novels from *Under the Net* to *The Philosopher's Pupil.*

### Essays about Iris Murdoch

Ashworth, Ann. " 'Venus, Cupid, Folly and Time': Bronzino's Allegory and Murdoch's Fiction." *Critique: Studies in Modern Fiction* 23, no. 1 (1981): 18–24. Develops the iconography of *The Nice and the Good* in relation to Bronzino's painting.

## BIBLIOGRAPHY

Bradbury, Malcolm. "Iris Murdoch's *Under the Net.*" *Critical Quarterly* 4, no. 1 (Spring 1962): 47–54. Argues that the story of Vulcan, Mars and Venus provides a loose framework for *Under the Net;* also discusses Murdoch's Jamesian style.

Fletcher, John. "A Novelists's Plays: Iris Murdoch and the Theatre." *Essays in Theatre* 4, no. 1 (1985): 3–20. While Murdoch can be considered a great novelist, her plays, with the exception of *A Severed Head*, have not been successful adaptations. The article considers, in detail, the adaptation of *A Severed Head* for the theatre.

Jefferson, D. W. "Iris Murdoch and the Structures of Character." *Critical Quarterly* 26, no. 4 (Winter 1984): 47–58. Murdoch's best novels (*The Sacred and Profane Love Machine*, *A Word Child*, and *An Accidental Man*) produce structures of characters which become part of the structure of plot (i.e., the narrative structure of *A Word Child* is divided into days of the week and their rituals).

Meidner, Olga MacDonald. "Reviewer's Bane: A Study of Iris Murdoch's *The Flight from the Enchanter.*" *Essays in Criticism* (Oxford) 11, no. 4 (October 1961): 435–47. Discusses themes in *The Flight from the Enchanter,* including the feelings of displaced persons, family relations, and the nature of evil.

*Modern Fictional Studies* 15, no. 3 (Autumn 1969). Iris Murdoch Special Number. Eight critical essays on the earlier novels, a note on the Murdoch manuscripts at the University of Iowa Library, and a selected checklist of Murdoch criticism.

Moss, Howard. "Narrow Escapes: Iris Murdoch." *Grand Street* 6, no. 1 (Autumn 1986): 228–40. Critical assessment of Murdoch's works, especially *The Philosopher's Pupil*, *The Sea, The Sea*, *Nuns and Soldiers*, and *The Good Apprentice*, in which various characters have intentions of remaking or recapturing the past and search for the Good.

## BIBLIOGRAPHY

O'Connor, William Van. "Iris Murdoch: *A Severed Head.*" *Critique: Studies in Modern Fiction* 5 (Spring-Summer 1962): 74–77. Discusses the characters in *A Severed Head* as amoral and calls Murdoch "a kind of twentieth-century Congreve."

O'Sullivan, Kevin. "Iris Murdoch and the Image of Liberal Man." *Yale Literary Magazine* 131 (December 1962): 27–36. Critiques Murdoch's first six novels on the basis of her own aesthetics.

Sturrock, John. "Reading Iris Murdoch." *Salmagundi* 80 (Fall 1988): 144–60. Discussion of love, freedom, and realism in Murdoch's novels.

Wall, Stephen. "The Bell in *The Bell.*" *Essays in Criticism* 13 (July 1963): 265–273. Claims that the meaning of the bell is relative to the perspectives of the characters. The main themes of the book are the conflict between sacred and profane love, the innocence and experience in spiritual life, and the importance of self-knowledge.

# INDEX

This index does not include references to material in the notes.

## INDEX

## INDEX

## INDEX

# INDEX

## INDEX

# 215

## INDEX

## INDEX